Soul Mates and Twin Flames

Attracting in Love, Friendships and the Human Heart

Kevin Hunter

Warrior of Light Press

The author of this book does not dispense medical advice or prescribe the use of any technique as a form of treatment for physical, emotional, or medical problems without the advice of a physician, either directly or indirectly. The intent of the author is only to offer information of a general nature to help you in your quest for emotional and spiritual well-being. In the event, you use any of the information in this book for yourself, which is your constitutional right, the author and the publisher assume no responsibility for your actions.

Warrior of Light Press
www.kevin-hunter.com

Body, Mind & Spirit/Angels & Guides
Inspiration & Personal Growth

PRODUCTION CREDITS:
Project Editor: James Szopo

Content in *Soul Mates and Twin Flames* is taken from the books, *Warrior of Light: Messages from my Guides and Angels*, *Empowering Spirit Wisdom* and *Darkness of Ego*.

ISBN-10: 0615925677
ISBN-13: 978-0615925677

Acknowledgements

Thank you to my spiritual posse that consists of God and my personal sports team of Angels, Guides, Archangels and Saints. Thank you also to Archangel Chamuel, Archangel Raphael and the Romance Angels.

Chapters

Chapter 1
Soul Mates ____ 1

Chapter 2
Twin Flames ____ 16

Chapter 3
Karmic Relationships ____ 28
Dysfunctional Relationships ____ 30
Reconnecting with a Past Ex ____ 34

Chapter 4
The Human Heart ____ 37
Ask For Help in Finding a Soul Mate ____ 40

Chapter 5
The Power of Love and Relationships ____ 50
Messages On Love ____ 53
Chemistry ____ 59
Invite Love Into Your Life ____ 64

Chapter 6
The Secrets to Successful Relationships ____ 7

Chapter 7
Stages of Coupledom ______ 78
Dating ______ 80
Casually Dating Vs. Exclusively Dating ______ 83
Boyfriend or Girlfriend ______ 85
Relationship ______ 86
Marriage, Civil Union, Commitment Ceremony ______ 93

Chapter 8
The Ego's War on Love ______ 97

Chapter 9
Bring Back My Lover ______ 107

Chapter 10
Getting Over an Ex Lover ______ 114

Chapter 11
Soul Connections ______ 124
Long Distance Relationships

Chapter 12
Friendships Change As You Evolve ______ 135
Loneliness ______ 140
We Are All Teachers ______ 145
Dissolving Friendships ______ 146

Archangel Chamuel and Archangel Raguel ______ 155
Spirit Guides and Angels ______ 157

WARRIOR OF LIGHT POCKET BOOK SERIES

Spirit Guides and Angels
Soul Mates and Twin Flames
Raising Your Vibration
Divine Messages for Humanity
Connecting with the Archangels
The Seven Deadly Sins
Love Party of One
A Beginner's Guide to the Four Psychic Clair Senses
Twin Flame Soul Connections
Attracting in Abundance
Abundance Enlightenment

♥

A Word

Soul Mates and Twin Flames is a mini-pocket book and part of a series of *Warrior of Light* books. Some of the content in the mini-pocket books are disbursed throughout three of the bigger *Warrior of Light* books called: *Warrior of Light: Messages from my Guides and Angels, Empowering Spirit Wisdom* and *Darkness of Ego.* The exception is the book, *The Seven Deadly Sins.* The bigger *Warrior of Light* books contain a variety of information within the spiritual empowerment genre. The reason behind releasing five separate mini-pocket books is for those who just want to read about one specific topic and are not interested in the rest. For example, all content geared towards abundance, the law of attraction, and fine tuning your soul related would be in the mini-pocket book called, *Raising Your Vibration.* Rather than having to buy all three big books to read about the information in each of them, you have it all in one mini-pocket book.

Author's Note

All *Warrior of Light* books are infused with practical messages and guidance that my Spirit team has taught and shared with me revolving around many different topics. The main goal is to fine tune your body, mind and soul. This improves humanity one person at a time. You are a Divine communicator and perfectly adjusted and capable of receiving messages from Heaven. This is for your benefit in order to live a happier, richer life. It is your individual responsibility to respect yourself and this planet while on your journey here.

The messages and information enclosed in this and all of the *Warrior of Light* books may be in my own words, but they do not come from me. They come from God, the Holy Spirit, my Spirit team of guides, angels and sometimes certain Archangels and Saints. I am merely the liaison or messenger in delivering and interpreting the intentions of what they wish to communicate. They love that I talk about them and share this stuff as it gets other people to work with them too!

There is one main hierarchy Saint who works with me leading the pack. His name is Nathaniel. He is often brutally truthful and forceful, as he does not mince words. There may be topics in this and my other books that might bother you or make you uncomfortable. He asks that you examine the underlying cause of this discomfort and come to terms with the fear attached. He cuts right to the heart of humanity without apology. I have learned quite a bit from him while adopting his ideology, which is Heaven's philosophy as a whole.

I am one with the Holy Spirit and have many Spirit Guides and Angels around me. As my connections to the other side grew to be daily over the course of my life, more of them joined in behind the others. I have often seen, sensed, heard and been privy to the dozens of magnificent lights that crowd around me on occasion.

If I use the word "He" when pertaining to God, this does not mean that I am advocating that he is a male. Simply replace the word, "He" with one you are comfortable using to identify God for you to be. This goes for any gender I use as examples. When I say, "spirit team", I am referring to a team of 'Guides and Angels'. The purpose of the *Warrior of Light* books is to empower and help you improve yourself, your life and humanity as a whole. It does not matter if you are a beginner or well versed in the subject matter. There may be something that reminds you of something you already know or something that you were unaware of. We all have much to share with one another, as we are all one in the end. This book and all of the *Warrior of Light* series of books contain information and directions on how to reach the place where you can be a fine tuned instrument to receive your own messages from your own Spirit team.

Some of my personal stories are infused and sprinkled in the books. This is in order for you to see how it works effectively for me. With some of my methods, I hope that you gain insight, knowledge or inspiration. It may prompt you to recall incidents where you were receiving heavenly messages in your own life. There are helpful ways that you can improve your existence and have a connection with Heaven throughout this book. Doing so will greatly transform yourself in all ways allowing you to attract wonderful circumstances at higher levels and live a happier more content life.

~ Kevin Hunter

Soul Mates and Twin Flames

Chapter One

Soul Mates

Everyone is interested in love and relationships whether they like to admit it or not. Even the most hardened human soul has fantasized about having a love interest, companion or a partner in crime. One of the main reasons all human souls are here is for the sake of love. This can be to learn to love or to exude love. All roads must lead to love in the end. This is not only in intimate relationships, but with everyone you come into contact with. You must accept someone else's differences in the way they choose to set up their life, as long as it is not harming someone else or themselves. It is in the core makeup of all human souls to want to help others out of love even if it is in the form of tough love. This love message was demolished somewhere along the way within in the human soul's upbringing. It is one of the major damages that the human ego has caused on the planet.

Relationships have grown complicated over the years. Society has imposed particularly rigid values and rules when it comes to how relationships should be. There was a time when interracial marriage was banned. Now there are laws on the books allowing same sex couples to marry, or the law is attempting to ban them from marrying. There was a time when divorce was seen as sinful and you would be permanently ostracized by society. If you committed adultery, you would have to wear the scarlet letter "A" for adultery as you made your way into town, so everyone could see that you committed a big no-no. You were forced to walk in shame upon judgmental and critical eyes. Divorce and adultery still go on today, but you're not forced to wear a button that says, "I'm a cheater."

Cheating is still frowned upon, as it brands someone's character as untrustworthy. Most human souls hope that someone they're intimately involved with can control themselves and be trusted not to stray. You cannot be with someone around the clock even if you live with them. The angels are egoless, and therefore do not judge someone who has cheated and nor do they brand them with a label. They see the underlying cause within that individual that prompts them to stray. They want to assist them in healing the source or fundamental origin that leads that person to seek out false fulfillment in toxic or harmful ways. They can only do so when that person has acknowledged that they desire help. If the human soul feels they are doing nothing wrong, then there is little your Spirit team or anyone else can do to help them. Make an outpouring request to the universe that you need some assistance and intervention. An angel or guide will enter the picture and work with you in ridding yourself of addictive temptations. Uncontrollable desires can cause hurt and pain in your relationships and ultimately to yourself.

Divorce is something that most cultures have come to understand and accept over the centuries. Your Guides and Angels will never urge you to leave your partner unless that person is emotionally, verbally, or physically abusive. They are about working on your union since there is no such thing as a perfect relationship. There will be times when you feel misunderstood, or are not being heard by your partner. This is your ego stomping its feet demanding attention.

When a couple hits a roadblock in their relationship, the answer is usually simpler than the human ego can see. The angels understand that some couples grow apart or stop seeing eye-to-eye. This is why they have performed miraculous interventions with couples that have reached a place where they are no longer speaking to one another. After the angels have intervened, that couple begins to see each other in a new light and are able to rekindle what they once had.

There are cases where there is no other solution within the relationship except to dissolve it amicably and peacefully. Every union's issues vary from one couple to the next. The bottom line is that relationships and love are a big deal to many people. You want to connect to others in a positive way and it disheartens you when it fails, or does not go according to expectations or plan. The angels watch you and your partner wrestle with hurt. They see the many miscommunications going on between you. The angels see the answer that can correct any misunderstandings and they want to help you see it too. Once you reach this place of understanding, then you achieve bliss within the partnership again.

There are those who prefer to be a lone wolf, but even they have moments where they wish there was someone in their life to do things with or communicate to on occasion. There are committed relationships that work where both partners do not live with one another, or they see each other irregularly. There are also many who prefer to live together almost immediately and often prematurely. Your Guides and Angels understand that it is a human need to want someone to share your life's journey with. This is why they work with those who request their help to bring in a loving, committed partner.

We all have certain requirements in a relationship with someone else that isn't always fulfilled. For instance, you may crave a passionate sex life with your partner, while they look at you as someone to hang out and go places with on occasion. They may not be romantic or passionate, and nor have a desire for the kind of hearts and flowers love that you crave. This can ultimately end a relationship if this issue is not accepted or addressed. The way to avoid an ending is to accept that this is where you are both different and then put in an effort to meet the other one half way. If you crave that passion around the clock, then ease up on that need, while the partner that does not have a desire for it should put in some time to be passionate with their partner that wants it. If one or neither party puts in an effort over a prolonged period of time, then the relationship will become frustrated and end.

Bigger issues that cause relationship break ups are where one person wants children and the other does not. Issues can be worked around to an extent, but these types of major issues should be resolved during the dating process, rather than when you are knee-deep years into the relationship. Many jump immediately into a relationship without truly knowing who they are joining in with. Before I ventured into other territory in my work such as spirituality, I was writing about love, dating, relationships and sex. This is an area that I was born knowing about. With a heavy grasp of the human condition through claircognizance, I gained additional guidance and messages from my Guides and Angels. Because of this and through life experiences, I have successfully assisted and navigated many through the challenges and questions revolving around their love and relationship lives.

Soul Mates

Everything you do, and every choice and decision you make every second has an effect. This effect is what attracts particular circumstances and people to you. Look back on the course of your life and the decisions you made and take note at what the results were. See yourself in an objective light. This will enable you to discover what part you played in a specific outcome in your life, and whether that invited in something good or bad. Your ego blames everyone else when there is no one to look at for your unhappiness, but yourself, your thoughts, choices and moods. Sometimes you are in situations that you have no control over and are powerless, but in truth you are never powerless. You own your life and have complete control in the decisions you make daily. You may not even be aware of every tiny shred of decision making you do every day, but you are making them regardless of your awareness of it or not. The exception is a child who is under the care of an abusive parent. When you are in the grips of someone else, stop and be still, and connect to your Spirit team for the answers that will get you out of that situation. Ask them for help and intervention, then step out of the way and let them get to work on it. It's important to not just ask for assistance, but listen and tune in for the answers that are being delivered to you. The answers are not always immediately forthcoming, but you will eventually receive that heightened moment of clarity where you know it is divine guidance.

Heaven never ignores you as they are always communicating with you. If you are not picking up on their messages, then you might either be blocked or not aware that you have heard them. Sometimes you come to find that you already knew the answer. This is confirmation that you are receiving the messages accurately. You were unaware that was Heaven communicating those messages you knew all along. Ask your Guides and Angels to continue to show you signs until you know for sure what it is they are relaying to you, then always say thank you. Being grateful is an important part of manifesting.

You have more than one soul mate. You may want to meet your soul mate, but you may not be aware that you have already met several of your soul mates. Your soul mate can be a family member, an acquaintance, a business colleague, a friend or a relationship lover. Soul mates are put in your path for the purpose of your growth. You both have something to learn from the other one that will benefit the progress of your soul. You will also know if someone is your soul mate if they challenge you in a way that prompts you to make positive life changes. They may get you to take a good hard look at what you need to change in your life in order to be happier. They might push you to accomplish your dreams or positively improve your soul. One example can be if you are lacking in self-confidence, but then an employer pushes you out onto a stage in front of an audience to give regular speeches. Those speeches change the course of your life where you gain confidence and a new career in public speaking. The union was successful in that it pushes you out of your comfort zone to conquer your fears. This colleague is your soul mate who you were meant to cross paths with at that point.

The people you meet online for a shallow rendezvous, or who you pick up in a bar, are not to be confused with being your soul mate as they are a distraction delaying you from your purpose by negatively feeding a part of you that feels empty. This isn't always the case, but if you do meet someone in this way and something happens with that meeting that triggers a drastic life change in you such as permanently giving up alcohol, drugs or any other negative block or vice, then that person was sent to you for that reason. Soul mates can be the people you come into contact with for any kind of important positive connection that changes or improves you. They are especially evident in the form of a friend or lover as those types of soul mates may be in your life longer than others.

You may have witnessed certain friendships that were once tight drift apart. This is because the connection was made to get you to a certain place in your life, but then it fulfilled its mission. One of the two parties might have grown and evolved spiritually in some way, and the soul mate friendship achieved its purpose. That soul mate may have been brought to you to help you start a successful business and then you find that the relationship deteriorates after that. This can also be a sign that this person was a soul mate to improve you in a certain area of your life. This purpose benefits everyone involved in a positive way and then it is time to disband the partnership. You take away only the lessons and love while being grateful for that connection.

A soul mate can be a friend who had appeared for you during a rough time when you needed it most. They offered the compassionate ear coupled with profound wisdom that helped you heal and get through a negative circumstance more quickly than if you had to go through a rough patch alone. If that person was not around at that time when you needed it, then you know that you would have had it much harder. This other person had the benefit of being a teacher, counselor or healer to you in some form for that particular circumstance.

Soul mate relationships can be challenging in that they force you to examine yourself by holding a mirror up to your negative flaws. With soul mates, you often bring things to the relationship what the other one is lacking or missing. Every relationship you had whether good or bad was not only delivered to you for the purposes of your soul's growth, but you attracted them in through the Laws of Attraction. If you are covered in addictions you will attract someone similar or on your level. You will not attract in someone who is well to do and who owns their life. Why would a spiritually minded health conscious person be with someone who falls prone to a plague of addictions on a weekly basis? If you want someone who appears as if they are on a higher caliber than you, then use that opportunity to start making long-term improvements and life changes for yourself so that your vibration will rise. You will have a bigger shot at attracting that person you are interested in for good.

My guides have shared with me that: *"50% of the people in the world cannot be in a relationship even though they ask us for one. They soon realize they don't want to be chained or tied down. They don't want to have to keep answering to them texting, calling, letting them know what they are doing and why or where. You don't do those things because you have to, you do them because you love them and you want to. You don't want them to worry up all night wondering where you are. We laugh here because many of you do not understand this today. You want it, but then when you have it, you can't do it and want out."*

Everyone wants companionship, but I often hear many complain that it is difficult to find a suitable love partner. There are various reasons for this and some of them are:

- You are expecting unrealistic perfection.
- Sometimes the soul mate love relationship the angels are bringing to you is being prepped and not ready for you yet.
- Your soul mate could be going through a transition in their life that ultimately prepares them for you and then the meeting will take place.

- Your vibration has risen to a higher level of spiritual growth and you are repelling those you were once attracted to. Your Guides and Angels are prepping a new soul mate for you who will match that vibration.

- Your next soul mate might currently be in another relationship with someone else that your Spirit team knows will be ending eventually. They are waiting for that relationship to run its course before they orchestrate a meeting with you and that person.

- Often times a suitable companion was sent to you, but you or the other person denied it or did not act on it. Your decisions to deny it are due to Free Will. It's more or less back to the drawing board for your Guides and Angels to find another potential soul mate.

- You might not be in a place where you are ready for the kind of soul mate relationship your guides want to bring you. You have your own transition and growth to take place before you are ready for a real lifelong love partnership.

Times have changed and half the world does not value relationships the way they once did. Many may not work at these relationships when they are in them. They are out seeking impossible perfection. They are under stress or bathed in addictions unable to attract a proper soul mate or even keep that person in their life. You have some work to do on yourself so that you are more ready for this right person.

Ask yourself what you have to offer in a relationship. Often many wonder, "What will this person do for me?", but this attitude is incorrect. There needs to be giving and receiving energy being reciprocated in all relationships in order for them to remain balanced and successful.

It's taken me a long time to get into the cycle of giving and receiving. I am a natural giver and have been uncomfortable receiving. This created issues in my past relationships. When you give and overcompensate, then that creates an uneven connection. You need to give and receive which creates an ebb and flow of energy. The same goes for those that are always receptive or receiving gifts, but not giving back in any way, then that creates imbalance and blocks in the relationship. This does not only apply to relationships, but it applies to your life in general. Giving can be as simple as smiling or saying hello to a stranger in passing. It is essential that all relationships have a give and take. All relationships need to have a healthy steadiness of giving and receiving otherwise there will be imbalance. The energy needs to flow freely back and forth to have a successful relationship of any kind.

You can only attract in someone good as soon as you become good. Do a thorough self-examination of yourself and be completely objective so that you can find out what you are doing that is harmful to your personal growth. Do you fall into a daily negative pessimistic cycle of constantly talking yourself down that you are not good enough? Where are you going to meet these potential soul mates? Are you hoping they will show up at your front door? Are you hanging out in bars, clubs, or even on those nifty little phone apps disguised as a way to meet friends, but are sexually charged for fleeting moments with no-name suspects? You will not typically find a put together, well rounded, secure, stable, busy professional hanging out there. This is ultimately what you need to embody for a successful long term relationship. In those settings you will usually only meet one type of person and they are after one thing in the end. They are lonely and bored souls who are looking for addictive ways to fill up their emptiness and insecurities. They are not ready to be in a healthy, committed relationship. Even if you do find that something is developing out of that, it is rare that it will be long lasting. Soon they will be logging back online to "chat" with other potentials. It is not the place you would likely meet the one to spend the rest of your life with.

Do not go diligently searching for your soul mate. You will cross paths with them naturally at just the right time. All of the soul mates I have come into contact with whether they are friends or love relationships came to me when I was not looking.

Take your time getting to know this person

when they enter your life. Closeness and trust must be earned with new people instead of blindly and naively latching onto them.

When you merge in a relationship with someone new, then the real challenge begins. Everyone tends to present their best self in the beginning, but you can only keep that up for so long before your true colors begin to show. This can take about six months before you start to discover things about your date that you're not thrilled about. Everyone is flawed and those imperfections are magnified in a relationship. The real test when you're a couple is how you dance together and work peacefully through any challenges that arise. It's around eighteen months when you really know if the relationship is working. I would not recommend moving in with one another until you have been together for at least a year and a half. This is when the honeymoon blush wears off and you know that what you have is working or not. At that point make the gradual transition into merging your souls physically under the same roof if you both choose.

When the initial attraction to your partner declines you get lazy and the ego kicks in and wants control over the relationship. It is not the real you. The real you is when you experienced happiness as you were getting to know this new person. They reminded you of the love and joy you were initially born with. A relationship is not about having all of your needs fulfilled. It is about giving and sharing with someone else. It is about companionship and learning to love. It is about lessons and personal growth.

You cannot enter a relationship and expect it to be successful until you are experiencing contentment and peace in your life first. If you are blinded into believing that some perfect person is going to sweep you off your feet and then you will experience happiness, you will be sorely disappointed. The all-encompassing love you crave is your detachment from Spirit and God's love. Another person cannot fill that void or emptiness. They do not have that kind of power to give you an impossible love. They may fill it for a brief moment, but then you will be right back where you started as your previous feelings of unhappiness begin to rise again. This is why it is important to make your peace with yourself and your life first before you enter a love relationship. Be content with you and the direction you are headed and then will you begin attracting in soul mates at higher levels. You will be more apt to having a successful long-term relationship that goes the distance.

Chapter Two

Twin Flames

Your Twin Flame is the other half of your soul. Most people do not meet their twin flame in this lifetime. Twin flames are a higher form of a soul mate. For some, your twin flame is waiting for you on the other side. They are not sitting around idly waiting, but rather they are assisting you to manifest soul mates for you in this lifetime. If your twin flame is in the Spirit world, they do not want you going through life alone. They want you to have someone to share your journey with while you're here. If your twin flame has reached a high level of spiritual growth that has surpassed yours, they will already have moved onto the other dimension. You will meet them again when you cross over. You will not meet your twin flame in this Earth life if you have not reached a high degree of spiritual and personal growth. If you do happen to be in the rare category where you have grown spiritually and therefore come into contact with your twin flame in this lifetime, then you may find that it won't be easy for you both. The intensity you have for one another are extremely deep. It's that true saying: *'I can't live with you – I can't live without you'.*

There is often an age difference between yourself and your twin flame of about ten years or more. They may be from a different state or even country entirely having varying cultural beliefs and backgrounds than yours.

The connection between yourself and your twin flame is so powerful that often one of the two of you finds it difficult to pursue a relationship with the other. The passion for that person is so great that it can make one or the both of you uncomfortable. Instead they choose to date and get involved with other people that are ultimately meaningless to them. It feels easier to them to do this than pursuing the relationship with their one true twin flame for fear of getting hurt. They are unable to control the intense feelings they have for them. They cannot get hurt as they are meant to be with one another. They will continue to cross paths until they accept that it truly is destined.

While one of you is in these mini-relationships with these other people you cannot stop thinking about the one that is your twin flame. You are not aware that this other person is your twin flame, but your thoughts always lead right back to the person you are consistently drawn to over the years. It does not matter how much you hide it or convince yourself that you are happy with this other random partner you're not serious about. Your thoughts always wander back to your twin flame, but fear stops you from making a move. When you finally do come around, you find that your twin flame has put up a wall and is inaccessible for the same reasons. You are both seldom on the same wavelength of '*let's do this'.* When you both do decide to merge, you experience the kind of fireworks that last lifetime after lifetime. It may take several tries over the course of many years before you ultimately surrender to the connection. You accept it and become fearless.

Because your souls were split at conception, the pull to one another is unshakeable. This is not conception of your human birth, but your soul's birth. You will continuously be drawn to one another in this and other lifetimes no matter how much you resist it. If you keep on running into or crossing paths with this person over the years and you are both experiencing a heightened intensity that never wavers, then you may have met your twin flame. You will often find that you have strong feelings for this person over the years without it ever faltering. There can also be a love/hate relationship. This is not to be confused with tempestuous relationships, which are more Karmic.

You could end up getting married to someone else and yet you find yourself unable to stop thinking about your twin flame. Years pass and you are in another relationship that ends up in divorce or a commitment break up. During this time you continue to run into this twin flame denying that it's the one. If you have a reciprocated and deep attraction for someone that continues on for years, then this could likely be your twin flame.

You do not reunite with your twin flame until you have improved yourself and your lifestyle. However, if your twin flame has improved themselves and their lifestyle, but you have not, then it could still be your twin flame. You were brought to them at the right moment where Spirit knew you were close enough to grasp these changes. This would prompt you to begin improving yourself in the process to match their vibration.

You must connect with a higher power such as God and make yourself truly whole before you are united with your twin flame in this life, the next, or in the spiritual plane. This is why it is rare to meet them in this lifetime, as you are here for the purpose of spiritual and personal growth and to learn to love. If you reach that level rather quickly in this lifetime, then it is likely you will connect with your twin flame. You do not need to take a retreat in an Ashram to be spiritually enlightened. It is remembering who you as a soul are. It is being aware of everything around you, being a good person, and having integrity. The message and theme is in every spiritual, religious or philosophical book written: Love thy neighbor as thy self.

You can find someone you enjoy being with, have a connection and live with them your entire lifetime in a marriage union, and yet they are your soul mate and not necessarily your twin flame. It can be confusing when you first fall for someone and wonder if they are your twin flame. This is because you might experience an immediate deep attraction for someone you have just met. This does not mean it is your twin flame. You will know they are your twin flame if you have the same immediate deep attraction for them in five years as if you are meeting them for the first time. There is also an ever-evolving spiritual growth with the twin flame relationship in one lifetime.

The intensity never leaves with a twin flame. Going days without hearing from your twin flame starts to take its toll on the both of you. All you think about are being in the same room with them, seeing them, or even just falling into a hug, all of which are oxygen to you both. This is years after knowing them rather than weeks, which is everyone's expected behavior in the beginning of dating someone you first meet. You are not typically this intense with others or in any other relationship. This is a rare case where you find it to be unusually powerful and it continues to be so with that person.

Where a Karmic relationship may be negatively volatile, a Twin Flame connection is beautiful and compassionate. It is reciprocated between both partners. It is not negatively unbalanced the way a Karmic relationship might be.

When twin flames connect in the beginning it is not easy. The energy is generally too strong for one of the partners who may continuously sabotage it. They have not reached the level of spiritual growth that you have. You are close in understanding the nature of personal growth since you've both incarnated relatively at the same time, but generally there is a large learning gap, which contributes to one of you not being mature enough to both evolve together just yet.

When you are together it feels like home, but when you are away from one another, eventually your heart aches and you want to be near them again. You can certainly function and you're not bed ridden, but your thoughts keep wandering back to them. These thoughts reside in the both of you.

Twin flames are not an unrequited or one sided love. It will be as if you have been waiting for this person your entire life and suddenly everything around you makes sense. In the rare case that you meet each other in this lifetime it will be kismet and magic. You will both know this is it instantly without second guessing it. You will be drawn to one another like magnets. You will both gaze at each other as if you have known one another your entire current and past lives. You will immediately be attracted to one another decade after decade. Your energy and aura pulls you both together indefinitely throughout the course of your lifetime.

THE DEEPER LOVE OF THE TWIN FLAME

The Twin Flame is the highest and deepest form of a soul connection. Twin flames rarely incarnate at the same time, even though there appears to be a trend that many are searching for their other half twin flame soul. It is not the goal to find one's twin flame since they cannot be found. When it is time for a soul to connect with their twin flame while on its soul's journey, then it will happen naturally with no effort. This is similar to the image of magnet attracting in steel. Most human soul's twin flames are on the other side. Searching for someone who is not living on the Earth plane may result in prolonged disappointment.

Every single soul knows their twin flame personally, even if they do not remember them while living an Earthly life. Your soul is part of their soul. Your souls split apart breaking into two when your soul was formed and sparked out of God. This is like human twins who have formed out of the same egg. With that come the many similarities and natures between them. Those who have a twin sibling mostly do not always look identical or have exactly the same interests. Your twin flame does not look like you, but there will be a great deal of similarities and a huge bond, and attraction that never ceases throughout the course of your Earthly life. Remember it is not one sided as both of the twin flames feel this attraction and intensity for each other indefinitely. This is the case even if they temporarily separate or one of the partners flees out of a need for independence. Fleeing is common among a twin flame. Their ego will want to focus on more practical matters rather than succumbing to the depths of an intense love connection with someone.

On Earth, usually one or both of the twin flames are involved in positive spiritual or faith based pursuits. If one is more involved in it than the other, then the other soul will display growing signs that they're heading in that direction. They are likely the younger partner of the duo, but not always. This is a human soul who has evolved to the level greater than the superficiality of the physical world. This isn't to be mistaken with two people who are involved in religious pursuits which harm others through words or violence. The twin flame soul is highly evolved beyond hate filled dogma.

It is near impossible for twin flames not to merge together in a love relationship. It's too heartbreaking on both ends for them to be apart for too long after they've first connected. The twin flame connection can be a tough connection to bring together at times. Sadly some twin flames connections come together, break apart, come together and break apart and repeat. This is due to one or the both of their egos denying they're meant to be. One or the both of them may sabotage or pull away from the connection due to its intensity. Yet they manage to end up right back together months or even years later again. There's a cycle where they are two peas in a pod, then a period where they have little to no contact with another, only to be back in one another's arms years later. They wouldn't be able to function or continue on through life indefinitely without the other one. This is on both ends and not just with one of them. If it's just with one of them, then that's an unrequited love, karmic connection, or soul mate relationship.

There's nothing wrong with someone being a soul mate relationship over a twin flame. In fact, the soul mate connections are at times easier than a twin flame union. Soul mates experience friction as well, but twin flames are more intense and feeling oriented. This contributes to the additional difficulties. The friction with twin flames is in coming together. They have trouble connecting and sealing the deal. This friction is due to ego. Human souls grow uncomfortable or over emotional when feeling a heightened love attraction for someone who feels the same way about them. This goes beyond a physical attraction and into an unwavering deep soul attraction. The more insecure partner of the twin flame connection may end the relationship more than once. Sometimes this is to pursue selfish ego gratifying needs, yet their twin flame partner will always be on their mind, or will continue to surface in their mind indefinitely throughout their life.

Everyone is with their twin flame at some point on the other side before they incarnate on earth. Many souls come to Earth either as student or teacher. Earth is school and all human souls are in class. When you graduate, then you go back home where your twin flame is waiting. This is why it's rare for the twin flame to be on Earth when you are, because one of them is usually more evolved spiritually. If that's the case, there is no reason for them to incarnate into a human body, unless they agree to an Earthly life in the role of Teacher or Leader.

This would mean that if your twin flame has

also incarnated into a human body, they have done so as student. The Twin Flame mix on Earth is either Teacher-Student or Teacher-Teacher. This is also why there is often an age difference between both Twin Flames who are in a human body, since a student might likely be younger, but not always. This is additional friction compounded onto the two souls. In Earth years they are in varying levels of human development that rub against each other uncomfortably, and sometimes even human generational gaps. The exceptions are if the younger soul is evolving rather quickly and maturely, while the older soul is tolerant and patient with the level the younger human soul is at.

Twin Flames might also be from different states in North America or they might be from different countries. Think of the image of the actor/activist couple, Brad Pitt and Angelina Jolie who are twelve years apart in age and from different states. They incarnated relatively at the same time for the humanitarian purposes and fights they do together outside of making movies. Although they have an age difference common amongst Twin Flames, they fall into the roles of Teacher-Teacher as well as Teacher-Student.

A quick Twin Flame recap:

You have many soul mates and only one twin flame. Most people do not connect with their twin flame in this lifetime. Twin flames are highly evolved souls. Since you are here for the sake of growing your soul, it is rare that you incarnate at the same time as your twin flame. Your twin flame is the other half of your soul. If your twin flame passes onto the other side long before you do, they will wait for you on the other side. They may choose to be one of your guides in order to work with your Spirit team to place potential soul mates in your path. They help you cope and strengthen your soul so that you can continue on the rest of your current Earth life. They do not want you to suffer or grieve over your temporary detachment from them, especially since they are alive and well. You have other important matters to attend to while you are here. Your twin flame does not want you distracted from that because they are in a different spiritual plane. You connect with your twin flame in this lifetime if you are on a higher spiritual path or you have evolved. Your twin flame would need to be in this same space as well or at least close to it.

It's sometimes difficult for a human soul to comprehend or connect with their twin flame on the other side, even though they are without realizing it. To your twin flame from the spirit world, they're very connected to you more than you know. You will be with your twin flame soon enough. To them, your life is a blip that lasts one minute in the spirit world. You may feel the presence of your twin flame at times as they send love to your heart. Even if you are feeling love for a new soul mate in your life, your twin flame is playing a part in opening your heart up to that soul mate. Your twin flame can also be of the same gender as you. Twin flames are the deepest love relationships that last lifetime after lifetime.

Your soul does not always re-incarnate immediately if at all. The ones that typically incarnate are new souls and teacher souls. You and your twin flame choose the when or how you will incarnate on Earth together if it is intended to happen. You agreed to this particular design. You likely won't remember that now, but your memory is restored when you cross over. You will re-connect with your twin flame when you cross over if they are currently in the spirit world. They are one of the many souls that greet you as long as they're not already living an Earthly life at the time of your human death.

The souls that re-incarnate immediately are the ones that had an Earthly run just to have an Earthly life with no other purpose than that. Human souls that commit suicide will generally re-incarnate sooner than later. This is because they cut their life short before they could fulfill their purpose. They need to go back and finish what they started. They move through an incubation process where their soul is restored before that happens. No soul is forced to live an Earth life. They make that choice with their Spirit team. They usually want to have an Earth life as they have more perspective while on the other side than they would on Earth. There is an importance in terms of their soul's growth on Earth that is understood. Other souls agree to incarnate in order to be a spiritual teacher on some level. The spirit world understands the significance of improving one's soul, other souls, and God's planet.

Chapter Three

Karmic Relationships

Karmic relationships are usually ones where you are incompatible in every way with this relationship partner, yet you both cannot stop from making a beeline to one another. It's like an unhealthy addiction. The relationship connection is more negative than positive. The negatives are obvious because it is deliberately antagonistic. One or the both of you might be abusive in some way such as physically, verbally or emotionally.

There will be other addictions involved between you two such as you both drink heavily or do drugs together. Basically anything that clearly does not benefit your higher self. The problem is that many people are unaware that the relationship cannot be saved and it is best to get out while you can. They might know that something isn't right in their relationship, but they do not know that they need to get out of the connection. One of the partners may continuously want to save the other person. They protest how much they love their mate with their friends. Yet, their friends may narrow their eyes in suspicion wondering what their friend sees in this partner. All they hear from their friend is one drama story after another.

These stories are the kind where one partner is constantly cruel to them. Perhaps your partner is always belittling you or making snide remarks. Maybe your partner is cheating on you, or you are having obsessive thoughts that they are cheating, and therefore always confronting them and making empty accusations. Perhaps one of the partners is jealous to the point where they act out physically by starting violent fights. It's normal to display signs of jealousy from time to time, but displaying that emotion in a heated way on a regular basis can be draining and will kill the relationship.

This may sound like a soul mate relationship, but soul mate relationships are not violent, negative or antagonistic. There might be disagreements or minor bickering among a soul mate partnership, but a Karmic connection is more antagonistic than not. Soul mate connections offer assistance in your personal growth of a positive nature. This is where they make you an improved soul. Karmic relationships are destructive. Those in them tend to either stay in these types of relationships or are always attracting them in. The way to break this type of relationship is by learning from it and stopping the cycle. Be aware of the lessons involved in this kind of hurtful relationship.

Gather enough strength to end the connection. When you learn from it, you are in complete awareness of how being with someone like that is not good for your higher self. You also forgive this person when letting go of it. Change your way of thinking and living in order to attract a more loving human soul mate.

Dysfunctional Relationships

You attract in people that are similar to you. You will also attract in those who you must learn something from or teach to. I am not going to be attracting the bad drug-dealing user I was at age twenty-two. I always wanted to be in a committed, love relationship where I would grow and evolve with one person. By the time I was sixteen, I was ready to settle down. Of course it didn't happen quite so simply. I did not have a positive view of successful relationships as I grew up amidst adultery, violent and negative unions. Some human souls are flawed and operate with a dominating ego. Be fully aware of how you treat others as it should be with respect and love. Spirit embedded the true long-term view of love relationships in me at birth. Having grown up disappointed, I stopped trusting other human souls. All I desired seemed simple enough, and yet I could not figure out why that was incredibly difficult for most others to do. The basic necessities of life are love and security. The irony is that you seek those two things out from other people when they can be perfectly supplied by the one true source.

As a result of my upbringing, I grew to be suspicious of anyone who attempted to get close to me. I would create self-fulfilling prophecies while in a relationship, such as saying, "How long is this one going to last? How long before this person takes off in search of something else? I wonder what they want from me or if they have an ulterior motive." I came to the conclusion that was the norm. I soon realized I was attracting the same type of person into me repeatedly, and not everyone is the same. There are good people out there who would make a loyal, loving companion.

As a super, passionate, hot-blooded guy I would choose to get serious with those who were uncomfortable with being touched. When I finally did attract in a relationship with someone who was equally super passionate, then that person eventually strayed. My lack of trust in relationships did not help. The days where I was not with any of them, I would assume they were up to no good since they all ended up doing that anyway. I had to drop my guard and have faith that not everyone makes those particular choices. I had to find a way to stop attracting in the same types of characters. Anything less than compromise is unacceptable in a relationship.

My vibration had risen to a great degree in my mid to late thirties. I made a pact to never get involved with anyone who I considered less than my equal. The only exception would be if I was meant to teach them how to be in a relationship per my Spirit team's instructions. If this happens to you, then you will have to know the difference between someone willing to learn and someone who is uninterested in gaining knowledge, but instead antagonizes you. If they are not in it to learn, but criticize you, then it's time to end the relationship. You are in soul mate relationships to teach and to learn from one another. I reached a point where I decided to sacrifice myself by waiting for the right one, rather than being with someone purely out of loneliness or the desperate need for companionship. You can have companionships in friendships. You do not need to have it in dysfunctional love relationships. Some human souls are commitment phobic for fear of being in the wrong relationship when the right one shows up. Relationships are not perfection. You are meant to work at something together and learn the nature of compromise, support and compassion. There are no relationships that are 100% perfect.

I have been around the block more times than I can count. I have had more experiences than I would care to divulge in. This does not mean that there are not those who have done far more, but I am hammering home that it was quite a bit of experience. I have been out on so many dates and physical connections in my lifetime that I would never be able to tell you how many as it was off the charts. I was the serial dating King and I never asked anyone out. I figured if they wanted me bad enough, they would court and pursue me. I am not that unobtainable or difficult, because I would always meet the other person more than half way.

If they made the move, I graciously reached out my hand and pulled them in with me. In the end, I gained a degree from the dating school of hard knocks. Without intending to, I had mastered the art of relationships, dating and sex. This happened through my own experiences coupled with my instant knowledge on relationships delivered to me by my Spirit team.

When someone is having love troubles or questions, I am the one they contact in my circle of friends. I soon took those lessons and began teaching it professionally through writing and books. I always found it ironic considering that my own romantic relationships in the past were typically unsuccessful due to infidelity or instability with the other partner causing a drastic imbalance. I had to examine how and why the romantic relationships I was in were with someone who was up to no good. Add to that, they were swimming in addictions such as heavy alcohol or drugs. They were experiences at that time that I do not regret, because they served a major function in my growth and purpose. Despite the relationships ending early, I knew that it would be good practice for me to drop my walls. It was important to open myself up more to fresh possibilities and ways of interacting in new stronger relationships with more evolved people. Each of my love relationships improved over the previous one for that matter. It can take years of effort to stop the cycle of attracting in dysfunctional relationships. You can get to that place when you put in the effort. Do the work and make positive changes within and around yourself.

You'll become a radiant magnet attracting in a healthier relationship with a stable partner.

RECONNECTING WITH A PAST EX

Sometimes you cannot meet another potential partner if you are still hung up on a past love or an ex who hurt you. Ask your Guides and Angels to either help you release your ex, or mend the relationship if it is meant to continue in an improved way. Your Spirit team needs to know that you are absolutely ready before they can get to work on it. If you have a huge pull towards your ex that is not negative, but a lingering attraction, then there could be a couple of possible factors. You both merged together the first time prematurely and this is why it ended. One or the both of you were not quite ready to receive the relationship in the right spirit. Or one of you was rushing it before it was time while the other was moving too slowly.

It is not uncommon for people to re-connect with their ex only to discover that the relationship is better than it was before. They had time to live, learn, grow and mature. Another reason ex's get back together at a later date is if there were no threatening reasons for you two to split to begin with such as addictions, cheating or abuse. State clearly with your Guides and Angels to either release your ex, or if you are meant to reconnect, to allow that to happen that benefits all involved. This is in keeping that you are both healed enough to forge ahead with a new relationship with one another, or dissolve your love peacefully so that you can be open to the right soul mate relationship.

I had some residual emotional damage from all of my past love relationships and this had built a wall around my heart that required a monumental effort to scale. I guard my heart carefully and with good reason. If one wants to finally have the type of relationship that you crave, you will have to let your defenses down. You will have to know the person well to be comfortable enough to do that. The person you get involved with should have an openness about him or her that will allow you to open up to them on many levels. This knowledge will help you feel safe and secure enough to trust someone new.

When I went through my own major spiritual transformation, I had added, *"Please assist me in eliminating all of these toxic, dramatic, unnecessary relationships that are only hurting me, so that I will be completely free and clear to receive this great soul."* You do not want to be prevented from connecting to your soul mate because you are drowning in pain over your last one that hurt you.

I am a love addict and with that I have ended up in some serious jams in my dating life. I have found many to latch on to me like a snake to a vine as if I have opened them up in ways where no one has. I would often hear them say at some point, "I have never been able to open up to anyone the way I can with you." Naturally they would be falling in love, but I would not be in the same way. I adored them as I do all souls, but I did not experience that kinetic spark you have when you know this is a potential partner for you. I was aware of this pattern throughout my dating life. One of the main roles my guides have shared with me is that I am a love teacher. These prospects and suitors were meant to cross paths with me in order to learn how to open up their heart center Chakras. The gain I had with each of them was mainly to teach them about love while learning to accept that this is the position I am to exude. They were essentially a student and whether they were older than me or younger is irrelevant as it was the same class lesson for all. Age has no relevance when it comes to Spirit and Heaven. Those restrictions and fads are what human ego has imposed as socially acceptable or not.

Chapter Four

The Human Heart

Express love with those you come into contact with. Be aware of how you behave towards someone else. Many complain about what someone is doing to them. They do not take any accountability for the part they played. Be mindful of your own faults so that you can improve yourself and your life in the process. This is not to say that if someone is cruel to you out of nowhere that you are responsible. It is that you do not need to be a victim of someone else's cruelty. It is walking away from it and not allowing it to continue. You are not here to live carelessly and recklessly with abandon. Do not assume it is okay to treat people badly. Wake up and give yourself the occasional scrutinizing self-examination on how or where you are acting out inappropriately. Include how you are with strangers and especially those close to you.

This waking up realization is in the same vain as someone who drinks heavily and one day comes to the conclusion that they want to stop. "Admitting" is the first step to recovery, because then your focus is on cleaning up your act. You hit that awareness point when you are accurately receptive in receiving clear messages from your own Guides and Angels urging you to eliminate certain people or negative behavior patterns in your life. It is your Spirit team who has been nudging you all along, but your ego denied it wanting self-gratification to feed the emptiness within you. This is the point of higher consciousness where you are totally clear about your behavior patterns and your lifestyle choices. Growth takes time and does not happen overnight. If you are doing the work then people who haven't seen you in years will notice the positive changes in you. They will know that you are not quite the same person you once were, but you are better!

Everyone has their lists of wants and needs in someone they want as a partner and yet some of them are unrealistic. The one thing rarely seen on these lists is the word 'love'. How about: "He/She has to be able to love and give love." They might say they have much to offer and go down the list, but few fail to say, "I have a lot of love to give." Why do you want to be in a relationship if you do not feel you have much love to give?

I have been out there in the trenches coming face to face with the ego in others on a regular basis. Many do unless you are living in a quiet, rural or country setting where Spirits power is heavy and easily accessible. This is the term when you hear the phrase "power place" in areas such as the mountains or the desert. Wherever there is vast regions of nature and quiet will give you a good idea where to go to re-center and connect to your Spirit team. You can connect with them anywhere, but it is doubly effective when you are in calm surroundings.

You were born out of love and with the greatest capacity to love. Unfortunately negativity and ego-based thoughts like judgment, hate and anger take over. All of those negative thoughts and feelings stem from deep-rooted fear or addictions you're consuming. You need to have great strength to not allow yourself to be swayed by others or your own ego. The ego is strong and can overpower the more sensitive. Ultimately the sensitive are more powerful than the ego in the end. This is why you hear that love conquers all. People are afraid of being alone so they conform to their peers, their community, and family so as not to be an outcast. They go along with false friendships, relationships and acquaintances to keep from being lonely. They mistakenly believe that if they sell out and conform, then they won't have to be worried about being lonely. Nobody knows who you truly are in that state. You have been inauthentic and are putting on a forged face. Go it alone even if it means you will be alone. Do not compromise your integrity for fear of loneliness or being misunderstood.

Asking For Help In Finding A Soul Mate

Ask your Spirit team to work on bringing a soul mate partner to you. You can call upon a *band of angels* that is at times referred to as the Romance Angels. They are similar to the cherub angels one might find depicted in Valentine's Day greeting cards and memorabilia. Yes, they really do exist! They often work as a team of three's. It does not matter who you choose to ask for assistance as your request is heard and the right spirit guide or angel to assist you in your goal will come in to help. Asking God for help with anything is the ultimate go to power for your Earthly needs, including manifesting soul mate relationships. If you are calling out to your guide or angel you are simultaneously bringing in God. You can do this the same way you ask for their intervention for anything else such as mentally, out loud or in writing. I have found in the past that I would write them a letter describing the kind of soul mate I wanted, but I would neglect to be specific.

Every soul mate I was in a serious love relationship with in the past seemed to regularly hang out in the bars, the clubs, or other sketchy places that the average person might question. They would meet people there and some would even go home with them, or bring them home to their place, and even forge a short lived relationship! They would stray or date around and chat with other potentials while continuing to "hang out" with me. All of the people I romantically attached myself to in the past had exhibited this behavior at some point. This is what I was attracting into me. No doubt they were Karmic connections. I had to take a good hard look at who I was allowing in my vicinity and to put my foot down. The irony is I didn't meet any of them that way so I naturally assumed they had the same values I did. Since we are not as objective about our own lives the way someone else might be, a block is formed and you do not pay attention to the red flags until it is too late. By the time I was deep into these relationship scenarios, that's when it was revealed to me on how they spent their free time. It was always along the lines of what many consider to be up to no good.

I reverted back to my letter to my Guides and Angels and revised it by adding something like: *"This potential partner is not someone who hangs out regularly in the bars or the clubs, and nor do they go home with these people they meet through these avenues. This is someone who is not dating around, and in fact, is also like me in that they are waiting for the right one before uniting with just anyone, even if it takes years."*

It is important to be clear in your request, because your team may bring you the perfect soul mate, but then you discover things about them such as they are not passionate or romantic and that's a big deal to you. Or as I stated in my case, they are not out there searching and meeting other people. The right person for you is going to be sure that you are the one. There will be no confusion about that.

You need to compromise and accept certain issues about your partner. There are also some things that you know you absolutely will not tolerate in a partner, such as they smoke cigarettes. The things I suggested for myself are what many people want when it comes to a soul mate. We all want a solid, healthy partnership. I would have no problem sitting in a lounge with the one I am with for a glass of wine or a beer. It is another thing if that person I am with is at the bar alone regularly or meeting new people that way. There is a fine line between both and yet it is important that you do not jump to conclusions even though what appears on the surface might be questionable. Sometimes having a conversation can clear things up before it turns into unnecessary drama.

When looking to get into a serious relationship with someone, you do not want to end up with someone who is not ready for a real relationship where there is no out. You cannot be with someone who needs to have an escape route or who is commitment phobic. Many souls have experienced this with others they cared deeply for, or they may have been that way themselves. I can attest that I have and so have my suitors. Even though that person might tell you differently and that they just haven't met the right one. The truth is they are not ready and will find excuses to avoid settling down. They equate settling down to losing their edge. On the contrary, the right loving, committed relationship is exciting and beautiful. It is true that not everyone is meant for a committed love relationship, but those that are not meant for it have trouble experiencing deep connections with other souls in this lifetime. It's generally fears that they will be tied down. They want to continue "having fun" in the form of feeding their toxic appetite. This is where their soul's growth is, which might be inferior to where yours is on the scale of personal growth. You cannot force, bully or trick someone in that space to be your marriage partner.

Write a letter to God and your own Spirit team of Guides and Angels pouring your heart out about what traits you are looking for in a romantic partner or friendship. Let them know what you will not be okay with. Ask them to bring you together and to give you the courage to speak to each other when you cross paths. This is important because how often do you find that you are attracted to someone who feels the same way you do and yet you are both silent and afraid to say hello? You end up passing each other like two ships at sea. Some do not realize that the one for them has been in front of them all along. This is because they might be addicted to the adrenalin rush that comes with pining over the wrong one. They may be disillusioned to believing that there is something better out there. They may still have some things to work on within themselves first before they can attract in the right person.

The stable love interest that comes into your life is actually the one that is more likely to be the one for you. They may seem nothing like you would typically be attracted to. Perhaps they might appear on the boring side or too domesticated at first. The truth is that the excitement of chasing someone who appears to be immediately electrifying is actually wrong for you. You are chasing after a mirage and therefore ultimately get burned or disappointed in the end due to their instability and ability to not commit. The often less glamorous choice is generally the one that turns into a real and lasting love relationship. This isn't to say that you are settling for a life of boredom. In fact, it's the opposite with the right one! Your Spirit team knows that you might crave a certain type of relationship with one person. This person is loyal and disciplined, and yet is also powerfully passionate in the bedroom. Ask and you shall receive!

I would go back to my relationship request letter to my Guides and Angels and continuously revise it. Naturally the letter grew to be a couple of pages long. After being disheartened by another suitor's behavior choices, I would add additional things like: *'It is mandatory that this person be loyal, loving, and compassionate. They must know the value and rewards of building a slow and steady long-term relationship that has security and friendly companionship.'*

You would think that those would be obvious traits in a partnership, but you would be surprised how often it is not. You might want to end your letter and request with, "This – or something better God." You do not want to limit yourself from being with someone that your Spirit team knows you will enjoy more. I still ask that we be attracted to each other knowing that this is a given anyway. You are not going to run off with someone you are not attracted to. There is a difference between lusting over a good-looking six packed Barbie doll model and someone that you have true feelings for their soul.

You might also be delivered someone who is attractive to others, but you find that you are not attracted to them until you get to know them over time. There are endless cases where couples admit that they were not initially interested or attracted to the person they are currently in a long-term relationship with. This is real love which grows over time, whereas fleeting love is one where you are immediately into someone for a couple of weeks only to have the feelings die off leaving you feeling dejected. The younger you are, the more likely you are attracted to something immediate that has no substance in the end. This is because you are lacking in life experience, maturity and knowledge to appreciate someone's true soul and character.

Since being passionate, romantic, giving and intimately sexy are a big deal to me, I would add that into my letter as well. I even added that I want a highly charged sex life with this one person. For me being physically touched and kissed repeatedly is oxygen to me. I have been this way my entire life and it's not going to change. I am a walking love bug, which can be a handful or detrimental to my well being state if I put it in the hands of the wrong suitor who is passion-less, unromantic, or non-committal. This is the same endorphin releasing I get through exercise.

Touch has therapeutic benefits that promote a healthy body. If you are someone who is not particularly passionate and are interested in being with someone who is romantic and always touchy feely with you, then this is an important detail for you to put into that request. You do not want to have a suitor delivered to you who is always showering you with kisses only to find that it continuously gets under your skin prompting you to pull away. You both end up suffering and the relationship crumbles. It may lead one of the partner's to seek out what's missing in their relationship with someone else. This is never advised, as you should always mend the relationship and work on it first. If all possible angles have been established and you have both come to the realization that neither of you have been happy after a long period of time, then dissolve the union peacefully.

When I had previously made my dramatic spiritual change and growth I had to add an extra detail to my letter that was not there before. It had to be revised so that I could request that this person be spiritual in nature or spiritually minded. This person does not have to practice it or even understand it, but this is a big part of my life. If I can't talk about it for fear of being judged, then it is not going to work with that person. If I'm with someone who attempts to continuously debate it, then I'm with the wrong person. It's safe to say or request that this person be spiritual themselves or at least be open minded, accepting and supportive of it. I am walking the talk and living as healthy of a life as I can. If I find myself involved with someone who is out partying all night, then I've made a mistake in what I have attracted in. That was my former life that attracted in those types of characters and I am no longer attracted to that. I cannot fake interest because we are two different types of people with different values and lifestyles. I have had enough experience to know to pull out of the connection immediately if I suspect something that no longer jives with my values.

My letter and request would eventually grow into several pages long wrapped with layers of detail. I am using what I have done as an example of how trivial it might seem to someone else, but to you it is not. These are things you enjoy doing. You want to be able to do them with this one person in a relationship. You are also manifesting this and attracting it to you by writing it out in a letter similar to a vision board.

I would add extra colorful things to this letter such as this person must be nice, caring and stable. They are someone to relax or have fun with. Sometimes we go out for date night once a week, while other times we are perfectly content to stay at home and watch movies entangled on the couch or on the bed together. We are developing something meaningful over time. It is someone who does not date much, but has mainly been involved in long-term relationships.

This person has not had many romantic relationships or dated around. The reason for this is those who tend to date around quite a bit, or who are having several mini-relationships that only last an average of a couple of months, are more likely to be unstable and non-committal. If they had done this in an earlier part of their life as I had, then that was who they were then, but not who they are now. Those who are not dating around are careful in choosing a mate, because they take the process and that person seriously. They are investing themselves and their life with this person and expect the same in return. They are completely ready for something real and tangible with someone else.

When I had my major spiritual transformation, I was no longer going out with anyone and everyone who showed the slightest interest. This would deem impossible anyway considering that I receive messages in abundance regularly. I made a pact to move towards those who practiced a healthy lifestyle as well as positive thinking. This eliminated about 99% of them! You can get a good grasp of the circles I was travelling in. Besides the typical wear and tear, peaks and valleys of relationships in general, I know that there will be issues every now and then in any relationship. The problems that arise with myself and the one I'm with will be tepid. We will work through them swiftly and always make up immediately if there is a minor rift that pops up.

Write a letter to your spirit team of guides and angels that includes what you're looking for in a partner. You may choose to include in this letter that the potential mate be physically attractive to you, but remain open minded to how this soul mate will appear. This can also work for career, health or anything else you desire. You're merely having a one on one dialogue with your spirit team. It doesn't matter if you hand write it or type it into an email and send it to yourself. What matters is the feeling and intention behind the letter.

Reading the letter to your Spirit team every day is not necessary. If reading the letter everyday to them gives you added optimism by partaking in that additional step, then that's fine too. It would be a personal preference, but not mandatory. Write the letter and then release it to Heaven. Those who enjoy cooking might pick up a cooking recipe, but then will start making slight changes to that recipe so that it works for them. This is the same concept as when you take on a suggested formula such as writing a letter to your Spirit team. Follow your gut on what feels right for you and trust that.

Remember to step out of Heaven's way once you've released the request to them. There is no time limit on when a soul mate will be delivered. It can be weeks, months, and even years, but the point is to not lose hope. In the meantime, get into the fun and joy of your life with positive activities. This will help you shine with radiance, which attracts in potential soul mate interests shifting in and out of your vicinity.

What I have described is an example of what you can put into this letter to your romance angels or guides. You do not want to forget the details because you would be surprised that the angels fulfill your request as you have asked. You finally meet and connect with this wonderful person who exudes the qualities you asked for, but then they display a negative trait you forgot to mention. Start bringing more love into your life today by exuding and displaying those traits yourself too.

Chapter Five

The Power Of Love and Relationships

The only thing that matters in the end is love. It is the #1 reason you are here. All souls have this love gene within them. Everyone has the gift and ability to love and express love, yet so many stop living in this space full time. They give or expect love with peculiar conditions behind it. If you do not feel love or do not have any love to give, then take steps to elevating your consciousness. Do not allow the wrath of your ego to dominate your behavior. The ego has no love. Any love that it does show has an ulterior motive behind it. This motive aligns with qualities such as greed or betrayal. It will crush your spirit and turn you into something cold - which is also a front. I have witnessed this happen in others where past circumstances have caused them to shut down from giving and receiving love. They are unable to be intimate in their relationships or in friendships. This is unfathomable to me. Love and joy are the highest vibrations that exist. Love is the nourishment that keeps your soul riding on cloud nine. It keeps you healthy and lucky in attracting in positive circumstances to you. Make a pact to live in the space of love full time.

A potential love partner comes to you when you least expect it. All of the serious relationships I have had in my past happened when I was not looking for it. Each one of them came about in the same manner. It did not happen when I was purging, in the middle of a change, or other major internal transformation. These soul mates showed up after I had gone through a mini-shift, which allowed me to experience peace. I was in a place of total contentment when every one of my romantic soul mates entered my life. As a love addict, I've always been consumed with an overflowing feeling of love. Growing up, I would use my pillow as if it were the one I was with. I would daydream of falling asleep with someone and having a profound connection with them in a loving, committed relationship. By the time I was sixteen, I was ready to unite with a soul mate in a marriage for life. I am a love bug and place the bar high when it comes to all things love.

Before the days of technology, relationships lasted throughout the duration of the couples Earthly lives. People stayed together and worked at it. There was less materialistic ego getting in the way that has a habit of crumbling the connections today. There is no perfect partner and yet through my research and interviews with single people, I've discovered that many of them are seeking perfection. This is a time in the world that is dangerously fixated on the media, fads and sexually charged images. Newer generations learn about this instant gratification desire. Fed to them since birth, they absorb this illusion and ultimately meet disappointment head on. There is perfection created in the media and in these images. They display false interpretations of reality. This is with the use of great lighting, camera angles, make-up and hair people toying with the one in front of the camera to make them look out of this world. Having worked in the entertainment industry for a good chunk of my life, and raised in the business, I have seen how they orchestrate everything to create the perfect shot. Most people have admitted to touching up their own "selfies" before posting those photos on social media. This is connected to self esteem issues that have risen in astronomical numbers in others due to the internet's perception that everyone must be picture perfect. What happens when you meet these picture perfect photo people in person for the first time? Both of you are not exactly what you expected each other to look like and therefore you've wasted one another's time. The sole reason you met them to begin with was you expected a flawless appearing human being who looks as if they jumped right out of a fashion magazine.

All souls are shifting in and out of each other's lives for numerous purposes. Soul connections made have no set period in how long they last. They might last a week, months, years or even a lifetime and beyond. Some come into your life so that you can learn important life lessons that prompt you to change and grow. This is where the connection might be a challenging one, but in the end it enhances your soul pending you learn valuable lessons from the connection. It must happen or you would not be ready for the next big step. You connect with that person in order to join forces with them on a particular quest or to gain specific knowledge. They may be your soul brother or sister. You connect through several lifetimes sometimes just to say hello.

MESSAGES ON LOVE

Sometimes you overlook the potential suitors sent your way. They may not be the kind of person you were expecting so you do not bother with getting to know them. You do not feel like you have a shot. When you run into this person, you instead avoid them. Your own Spirit team sets up these chance encounters. They work together with the other person's guardian angel and spirit guide in order to orchestrate a meeting or a place where you will both cross paths. They will not bring a romantic soul mate into your life to replace your current one. If you meet someone while with your current mate, this does not necessarily mean your Spirit team sent this person. Heaven is about working it out with your current mate before considering bringing another into your life. Your current relationship would have to end. Time would need to be spent working on yourself afterwards before a new soul mate is delivered to you.

There is one exception. For some, they have a lifelong soul mate or twin flame relationship that will come to them regardless if they are already in a relationship. This is because you and this other soul chose to meet at such and such time no matter what. It was set up and designed long before you were born into an Earthly life. You will know this is the soul mate if you end up with this person for the duration of both of your Earthly lives.

It can be challenging, because many people do not follow the guidance of their Guides and Angels and may be more prone to act on free will. There will be times where you or this other potential does not happen, because one or the both of your egos refuse it. Your Spirit team will continue with the search of putting other potential possibilities in your path hoping you both notice each other and strike up a conversation. They will at times continue to put the same person in your path for months and maybe even years trying to get you two to notice one another if it is indeed meant to happen this lifetime. This is why some couples have later recounted that after they became acquainted with one another they indeed had some near misses. They discover they had many missed encounters where they would have been together much sooner if it were not for their ego denying it or the fault of poor timing. Perhaps they were at the same store location, but missed each other by a couple of minutes. They can be the two people who work in the same building together, but continue to miss one another in the lobby and elevator by mere minutes. These unforeseen circumstances cause long delays between soul mates meeting and uniting. You and your potential soul mates Guides and Angels can only maneuver and control so much in order to get you two to connect. It's challenging for them to work on delaying or speeding up morning traffic in such a way that you both manage to arrive at the work building at the same time. They do indeed perform these brilliant miracles, but this is to illustrate the amount of challenging circumstances they have to move around to get you both in the same elevator together.

I receive questions from others regarding personal psychic or angel reading sessions they had with a reader. Sometimes the question might be regarding messages they received from their own Guides and Angels. One of the questions is they are told that they are meant for a specific person in a relationship, but that the person in question is already involved with someone else. The answer is an easy one. He/she may not last with this other person. When it is complete, then you will both cross paths and merge, pending that no other circumstances have taken place with either party. Two human souls who are meant to have a soul mate connection with each other will cross paths with one another repeatedly over a lengthy period of time until they finally notice one another and take action. If they do not take action, there are several reasons for this below.

There are people who are supposed to meet each other and yet they never manage to connect in this lifetime. This is mostly due to free will. Most human souls have saturated themselves into the material world. The media, their peers, and society heavily influence their nature. This blocks the important messages and guidance coming in from the spirit world. This makes that person more susceptible to ruling from their ego. For that matter, they tend to act upon free will. When you act upon free will, then you miss the gifts and wonders that God is placing in your higher path including a beautiful all encompassing love relationship.

When it comes to two people connecting in a soul mate relationship, one or the both of you acts on free will and denies that the person they have crossed paths with is the one. Their ego convinces them that the soul mate potential is not what they are attracted to. They write off behavior patterns or habits this person does without giving them a fair chance. There are habits in others that are an understandable definite no such as they drink heavily, do drugs, stray, sleep around and hang out in bars regularly as a fixture. The habits I am talking about are much smaller and forgivable such as they did not return your text immediately that day. Or they are not tall, blonde and built to the nines. Your ego quickly writes them off, not realizing that this person is the one you are to connect with in this lifetime.

Before the media took over and dominated its influence on humanity, there was a courting process between two people. The couple in question was much more accepting of the other's idiosyncrasies and foibles. They also took their time getting to know one another before anything physical happened. This not only made the physical emerging sexier and hotter, but it also contributed to the longevity of their connection. The connections today are immediate and fleeting. This prompts many couples to split long before they truly know each other.

You cannot call one a couple or say that they are in a long-term relationship until they have been together for at least a year. Half of the couples that connect today do not make it that long. This creates a combination of loneliness and aloofness among souls whose basic nature is supposed to be love. This makes you grow cold and detached while continuing with your search for something instant to give you immediate pleasure and satisfaction. All the while wondering what it would be like to be with someone in a long-term marriage like relationship. Years pass and this pattern in your life increases to an astronomical and unmanageable degree. The image of this soul mate connection starts to take on a picture perfect vision that makes it even harder to believe it will come true. The person you seek and which you have conjured up in your mind has perfect qualities that no one in the world could fulfill. This perpetuates and delays any connection to any potential soul mate partner.

When you are in a relationship, be unlimited in love. I used to say that I was difficult in love. Due to my past relationship experiences, I assumed the love I demanded was over the top or outlandish to a degree because I discovered no one knew how to do it. The intensity is beyond what an ordinary human being can give, but those who are no ordinary human souls understand this. Sent here with our individual purposes that have the capacity to be far reaching, one can find disappointment in ordinary human soul love. Our hearts are just too big for our body to contain. The truth is the right one has the same equal belief systems, values and desires as you do. It is the same give and take. You cannot allow the quality and size of your Spirit to squeeze itself into a limited system of values. You are whole, perfect and full of immense love. Allow this to shine so bright that it attracts in the right mate for you. Be completely together much more than you realize! Get out there and continue to live life. Go to the places you want to go and do not allow anyone to stop you from living and loving. Let go of the need to control the need to know when the soul mate connection will happen. Trust it is evolving on divine timing.

Know that some soul mates are an awakener for you. This is by allowing you to experience the emotions and thoughts that you had unknowingly closed off. The soul mates purpose is to bring your true soul out of the human body to get some air!

CHEMISTRY

Having chemistry with another human soul is only the beginning of where it could potentially lead if anywhere. This is a comfortably, strong and deep attraction that is experienced by both people when they are together. Chemistry is a positive mutual, reciprocated feeling with another person. You cannot act on chemistry alone though. Having chemistry on a first meeting with someone is natural for any human soul who is connecting to the newness of someone you have crossed paths with. This does not mean it is meant to move forward beyond that. Chemistry can be a dangerous thing depending on the scenario. Human souls are always experiencing chemistry with other souls, but that does not mean it is a love relationship waiting to happen. You can have chemistry with your closest friends and that is all it is, a friendship.

There are many different levels of chemistry. There is the, "I just want to have sex with this person", chemistry. There is the, "This person really gets me on a friend level", kind of chemistry. A successful relationship experiences chemistry on many levels. You are physically attracted to each other. This person is also your friend. Drawn to one another you find yourself heading back to that person and they are drawn to you. Being with someone who is exactly like you in every way can lead the relationship to grow stale. This works for friendships that you communicate with on a regular basis, but not so much love relationships, which require some shades that are slightly different from your partner. The hues are not vastly different where it causes constant friction of course, but different enough that it continues to attract you to this other person. They are not quite like you, but there are elements about them that pull you in. Although it is important to have similar interests and values to an extent, it is even more so important that both parties involved in the relationship have some differences. This is somewhat close to the saying that claims opposites attract. The fine print version of the opposites attract syndrome is that they should not be too much of an opposite because then you will not connect completely. An extrovert can indeed be in a healthy long-term relationship with someone who is an introvert as long as they are facing the same direction. This is a case of opposites attract working.

One of the many reasons love relationships happen is for the sake of your soul's growth. For this reason, being involved in a healthy long-term relationship is beneficial when you are with someone who has some elemental differences than you. You will gain knowledge and lessons from this soul. It will also teach you to love someone who is not exactly like you. The relationship in general will teach you to work with others through compromise and communication. These are life lessons that build character and thus enhance your soul's growth. There does come a point where the differences might be too vast for a relationship to thrive. These are what might seem obvious in the realms of common sense. If someone is incredibly different from you on every level, then coming together might be impossible. This is not the case if it is a sexual connection. Human souls do experience the kind of chemistry that takes place with someone you are simply lusting after in a sexual way. Anyone that has partaken in such chemistry knows that it is short-lived and not long lasting. This is not to say you should stay away from that kind of connection. If you are one hundred percent single and alone, then there is nothing wrong with connecting in a physical way with someone you are having strong, intense feelings for sexually. Ensure you are being responsible and using safety precautions, but know that it will not assist you in finding the love you crave.

When strong feelings are involved, your dopamine levels rise. Dopamine is the naturally producing chemical in the brain that prompts you to display loving feelings. Being a Don Juan Casanova type myself, I have met no other who knows about breathing in this dangerous chemical full time. What is hazardous about it is if you target this love towards someone who is wrong for you. Having this feeling for someone you meet while currently with someone in a relationship is not for the right reasons. The Romance Angels say that taking off in search of greener pastures is like chasing rainbows that eventually fade. The love chemical in your brain can cause you to see things with rose-colored glasses. It is unsafe to your heart when you direct this towards someone who does not share this same love with you. While there is nothing wrong with loving love, keep some measure of a reality in check so that you do not get hurt.

When you have chemistry with someone at the beginning of getting to know them, you likely do not pay much attention to the red flags. Later when your union hits a wall of unhealthy issues, you look back in hindsight remembering how you did see the red flags. You failed to think much of it until you dove too deep into the connection. You might use the excuse of, "Well had I known this I never would've moved forward with the relationship. By the time I discovered all this, I was too emotionally attached." In truth, if you take a step back you might be able to hone in on where the red flags were apparent. It might've felt so subtle at the time that you failed to think much of it. Most human souls tend to have the rose colored glasses on when they experience immediate soul attraction to someone who is feeling the same thing. Rose colored glasses give you the great love high, but the mirrors of the glasses are fogged up to the point where the real reality is distorted.

If you are in a loving, committed relationship and a red flag pops up, that does not necessarily mean to leave the relationship. At that point, it is more about addressing an issue that is extreme enough to rock the foundation of your connection. Your partner is in the relationship with you at that point and should be open to working out whatever the issue is. If you notice they're flirtatious with others when you're out together, the chances are they were always flirtatious by nature. They don't suddenly become flirtatious way into your relationship.

Sometimes long-term relationships lose their chemistry, but if the couple was able to come together repeatedly over the course of time, then the chances are they can restore the chemistry and balance in the relationship. A long lasting relationship goes through highs and lows while they are together. They are fully aware they fall in and out of love with each other over the course of their life. Falling out of love does not mean hatred or leaving the relationship. It is having an understanding of the basic nature of the human ego, because your higher soul is all love and never falls out of love with anything or anyone. There will be periods of detachment between one another while in a committed relationship. Allow your partner the space they need and be willing to communicate about anything important. Knowing when the other person needs space is vital. The partner having a temporary moment of detachment could be going through a personal transition or transformation. The other partner senses this and grants them the required space, while remaining nearby should their mate need them. Any couple that takes their partnership seriously realizes that they may hit a wall where it feels as if the chemistry has evaporated. The partnership is strong and rock solid enough that one or both of them soon rise to the task to rekindle the fire that never truly extinguishes for good.

INVITE LOVE INTO YOUR LIFE

Over the course of entertainment history, there have been love songs recorded, romantic movies filmed, and books written about having a secure, loving and passionate relationship. Someone felt those things, craved it, experienced it firsthand or witnessed it in others. Love is a universal need. It is your soul's innate nature even if you lost the ability to operate from that space. You can find that space again because the love you were born with never leaves. You just bury it beneath layers of cement.

Many singles feel discouraged about love. They crave and desire it, but when pining for a wonderful soul mate has turned to years of rejection or no success, then it can cause one to become everlastingly disappointed. The Romance Angels say that remaining optimistic about love is what is going to bring you this love. I can attest personally that I understand how difficult that can be, but through work you can get there. Doing the work means catching yourself when you find that you are negative whenever it comes to the word love. Be aware when this happens and then shift your state of mind into something positive.

Think something like, "I am blessed with a loving, soul mate relationship." Say it as if it is already here. It's about believing that it is happening now, rather than it's going to happen. Nothing is going to stop you from obtaining it. Get into the joy of your life. Feel the feelings of optimism when it comes to all aspects of your life. This opens up your heart chakra to receive love. When you are playful, lighthearted, joyful, and allow your inner child to shine, then you will attract in wonderful soul mates to you.

One way to focus on love is when you head to sleep at night. You are lying down in bed as your thoughts drift. Allow your thoughts to move into a visualization of you in a relationship with the kind of person you envision yourself to be happy with. Picture yourself in the house together with the picket fence and the animals. Go all out and do not withhold for fear of it not happening, or that you are being what someone's ego might call cliché. This is about you. What do you desire? Allow your mind to play you this mini-movie of this relationship you seek. It may come to you quickly or it may take some time, but never give up on love. Love yourself and those around you more. Become more appreciative of having these loving thoughts.

You can purchase some Rose Quartz crystals and leave it next to your bed. You can also put it under your pillow when you sleep. Carry it in your pocket, car, or purse. Lie down on your back somewhere comfortable in meditation and place this crystal on your heart. Take a deep breath in and exhale, then repeat this step as you relax. Visualize the crystal opening up your heart and allowing love to pour into your heart. Envision this love pouring back out of your heart and into your love's soul light across from you. Allow the light to envelope the both of you. It is not necessary to have a specific vision of what this person looks like and in fact it will be equally powerful allowing them to be faceless. This means you're leaving the door open for the angels to bring you a soul mate who might be more amazing than you initially imagined.

Purchase some *rose essential oil* and dab it on your heart. This is beneficial when you have been feeling closed off from others. Breathe in deeply and see a magical pink light shooting into your heart from Heaven. Send this light out tenfold back upwards and out of your body like a geyser. It is not necessary to go all out and purchase Rose Quartz crystals or rose essential oil, but it most certainly will not hurt it. You can manifest what you want with the power of your own mind. Love will come. Love is here. Love is within you and always will be.

Love yourself more in order to open up the feelings of love within and around you. This can be in the form of self-love, which is admiring all that you are. Love how you physically appear. Strip down and look at yourself in the mirror and say, "I love my body." Buy yourself a gift as if you are buying it for someone you love. Watch a romantic movie, have a massage, some pampering at a spa, or take a mini-vacation somewhere. Dive into your hobbies that bring you joy. All of this is self-care, which not only opens up your heart chakra, but also assists you in bringing those love feelings to the surface. You glow in this state and other potential suitors or people on the street notice this. You are a magnet that attracts in love. If you are currently in a relationship, then this will add some extra love into your connection. Even more powerful is if your partner participates in this with you.

Keep in mind that sometimes the soul mate you envision or crave may appear in a different way. They might be right in front of you and yet you are not immediately noticing. This is because you have a specific vision of who you think they will be that you do not realize that this soul mate is already in your vicinity. They may not be what you were expecting and you might not even be completely attracted to them right away. There will be some measure of attraction, but it is so slight you write it off because you are not feeling all of the feelings you expect to happen with a potential soul mate. Those feelings grow even more as you get to know this soul mate. Keep an open heart and an open mind while on your search for a love companion. Release the need to know when or how this person will come to you. Find activities that make you smile and enjoy. This keeps your heart wide open. You will be so busy enjoying yourself only to discover your soul mate has arrived and you are having a conversation. Worrying about when or how it will happen darkens your aura, causes you grief, and prompts you to feel depressing thoughts. This does not make your light attractive to others and you certainly do not want to repel your soul mate from entering your vicinity.

If you have had a history of bad past relationships, use the time that you are single to make crystal clear intentions about what you will or will not accept in a loving, relationship. You will want to keep these needs somewhat flexible. If you are too rigid in your list, then you will repel the right soul mate for you. The kinds of things that are understandable of what you will not accept are things like, cheating, abuse in any form, alcohol or drug addictions, etc. The list would not include things such as where you insist that your soul mate calls you back immediately whenever you send a text. Controlling demands do not invite a loving, compassionate and loyal partner to you. It instead brings in a partner who exudes the negative traits you were hoping they would not have in them to begin with.

In this same respect, controlling your current relationship if you are in one creates a difficult situation. No one likes to be controlled or have harsh demands placed on their backs. If your current partner is behaving in ways that you disagree with or that do not jive with your values, then discussing it peacefully with them is the next step. If that does not work, then consider working with a couple's counselor. It also boils down to what you can live with. If your current partner is not abusive, or addicted to alcohol or drugs, and does not cheat, then put in some extra effort to work on the partnership before considering leaving. If you leave, you will find that you will be stuck with someone far worse than your current mate is.

When making a commitment to someone else, you are first making a commitment to you. This practice of commitment with your own self is what you will carry over into your loving companionship with your partner. If you are irresponsible in your own life, with your actions and decisions, then you are not quite ready to commit to another human soul. This shows if you have a tendency towards short-lived connections that have no staying power. Work on taking responsibility for your life, yourself, your soul and all of your surroundings. Making a shift in that direction where it becomes second nature to you is what will make it that much more effortless when joining with another committed, loving soul.

While in a relationship, avoid divulging every little tidbit that goes wrong with those close to you such as your friends. They may persuade you to leave a divinely orchestrated relationship. The natural reaction from those close to you is that they will side with you and not your partner. This is unfair to the person you are with. It will cause you more confusion when you are influenced by the words of those close to you. You have no idea what action to take if any. If it has come to that, it is best to take a time out for yourself and disconnect temporarily from your circle until you have individual perspective.

Loving relationships that run into roadblocks or a stalemate can deepen their connection by spending time alone together. This means getting away for a weekend trip or hiding out in your house and creating a romantic environment for just the two of you. When you spend time alone with your partner, then your feelings grow. This is extra beneficial for a relationship that has reached a point where one or the both of you feel stuck. This is what it means when others say relationships take work. You have to put in the work. You have to care about it. When you care about your relationships, then you care about you.

I am a firm believer of date night at least once a week while in a relationship. Inject laughter and fun on your date nights. It should be a relaxed and playful time for the both of you to forget any cares, stresses or worries around you. Love relationships have this benefit in that the right partnership is an escape from all negativity in the world. When you are with them, you remember what is truly important in this life. Love is all that matters. Loving relationships help you remember your divine heritage.

Chapter Six

The Secrets to Successful Relationships

Most human souls desire companionship on some level. You crave someone to be by your side that understands and supports you. Someone you champion and who appreciates you in return. For some, it might be a platonic friendship, for others it might be a sexual relationship with the same person throughout this lifetime. Your soul split into two souls at its original conception. This other half of you is your twin flame who many long for. They are a part of you, although not everyone connects with their twin flame in this lifetime. You move through this life feeling like there is something missing. In essence, you are searching for your twin flame. For most human souls, their twin flame is usually on the other side guiding you to healthy soul mate relationships for you on your Earthly journey.

Jaded singles have protested a myth that they believe those who are in relationships are unhappy. This could not be further from the truth. Those in unhappy or volatile relationships usually contain one or both partners who are not ready for a real relationship. They have not done the inner work yet. They bring their worst selves, their ego, and negative habits into the relationship, and then place that burden onto their partner. The connection is full of toxic energy that never lets up. The couple might be the type that argues more than they express love. It is normal to have a disagreement with your partner, but it is harmful if you are butting heads on a regular basis. Those who are in successful committed relationships are happier, healthier and more productive in their lives than those who are not in peaceful connections. The ingredients for a successful long-term relationship are vast.

One of the secrets to happy relationships is that both partners are open and communicative with one another. If you do not communicate openly, then how do you expect your partner to know what your needs are? How are you to work at it if your partner has no idea how you are feeling? Meanwhile, you are making plans that will affect your mate and they have no idea. It is not fair to leave the one you are involved with in the dark.

When you head to work or your job, you have to do more than show up. You actually have to do the work. Granted you are receiving money to do that work. Whereas in a relationship the payment you receive is the experience and lessons you gain with your partner that benefit your soul's growth. This is worth far more than any money earned. Money is temporary, while your soul lasts forever.

Another problem that can arise is that you or your partner feels uncomfortable or afraid to bring something serious up with the other one. This is not being assertive, but living in fear. You might fear that your partner will take it the wrong way or that they might attack you if you bring a concern up. If your partner always attacks you for opening up, then this is a red flag that you are with the wrong person. No one should have to endure any measure of abuse from anyone ever. If there is an issue at your job, most people have to bring it up unless they want it to blow up in their face down the line. If they do not bring it up, then disaster will hit. Someone will say, "This could have been prevented." Alternatively, they might say, "Why wasn't I notified?" In relationships, some couples are afraid to bring serious needs and issues up because they do not want to rock the boat. If you do not bring your concerns up or any potential issues, it is not going to go away. In fact, it will grow into a bigger problem resulting in more damage.

Your relationships are to be safe haven. You need to feel most at home when you are with your mate. You should be feeling safe enough to communicate openly and work through issues together by talking it out and taking action steps to mend what needs to be. Not being able to talk to your partner about anything is like walking on broken glass. This is no way to live a healthy and happy life.

You have been feeling suspicious that your partner is not being faithful. You do not want to mention this insecurity because you fear that you will be wrong. You worry that your partner will judge you, criticize you, get defensive or attack you for the accusation. This is not a loving partner. A loving partner is understanding and compassionate. They reassure you that there is nothing going on with anyone else and that you have nothing to fear. If your partner does become angry and defensive, then this can potentially be an admission of guilt. They are uncomfortable with emotional vulnerability and therefore not completely equipped to being in a loving, healthy relationship. On the other side of that equation, there is a difference between making a cruel accusation in anger and peacefully discussing insecure feelings. When you attack your partner, they will naturally become defensive and retaliate. All of this hostile energy flying back and forth, but no honest discussion with answers ever enters the equation. The ego of both partner's end up controlling the conversation leading you both nowhere, except more defeated and drained.

Those in successful relationships feel openly comfortable to discuss the touchy subjects such as vulnerabilities or insecurities in the relationship. They nip it in the bud immediately so that it does not grow like a dangerous, toxic weed in their beautiful garden.

Successful couples have similar values and interests to a degree. For example, both partners have a desire to live in the same part of town. You will run into problems if one of you wants to live in the big city around people, while the other prefers a quiet nature setting somewhere in a rural area or countryside.

If one partner feels like they cannot keep their feet planted in one spot and the other is perfectly at home doing that, then you will run into problems. There is a limit to how far compromise can go on some of these bigger issues. This is where communication is key once again.

Relationships are work and it is like a job in the sense that you both have to show up for the task. There are many couples where one is always on the go for weeks on end, while the other is at the home base. Is the one at the home base okay with this scenario? What if the partner on the go decides to take off and never come back? Is this who you want to commit to? There are billions of people in the world and it is impossible not to connect with someone who shares your ideals to an extent. You will find another soul mate potential with similar values as you have. This would include offering you more stability or reassurance that they are in this with you.

A successful relationship is facing in the same direction. It is joining to fight for everything around you together whether that is a parking ticket or having your partner's back in support.

Having or adopting children is another area where compromise does not always work. One of you wants or has plans to have children one day, while the other partner vocally does not or is flip floppy about it. This is where they protest that they want children, but then on another occasion they reveal they never had any interest in wanting kids. You are stunned to discover this truth. You could have sworn they were interested in having kids one day, while your partner is wondering how you ever got that idea in your mind. This type of person is flip floppy around many issues surrounding ones values. Flip-floppiness is someone who is not fully committed. They do not know what they want. Unfortunately, they are more or less stringing you along. You stay with them thinking they will change or that they need more time. Years in you come to the realization that they are never going to change or settle down. They have fears that govern their relationship lives and connecting with other people. This prevents them from being a grown up and mature soul. Fear is a relationship killer.

Human souls grow and evolve, but not always. Many stay relatively the same. When you were sixteen dreaming of a long-term committed relationship, this will not change when you are thirty-five. You more or less will still want that if it hasn't arrived or if you are newly single again. The only change would be that you grow more realistic as you age.

Trust is another important factor in a successful relationship, but more importantly is communication. Successful relationships endure because both partners communicate with one another and think of each other as the other's soul mate. Their love and understanding grows over time instead of fizzling out the way a fickle connection might. They are supportive of one another. They accept each other for who they are - imperfections and all. They work together in assisting in one another's growth. They shower one another with love and compassion. They are a beautiful and magnificent team.

Heaven and the angels love seeing two human souls in loving, committed relationships regardless of the genders involved. They know that once you are in a relationship that the real work enters the picture. They are by the sides of couples that request their assistance in empowering and improving the relationship. When there is friction going on or a disagreement between the both of you, then call on your Spirit team to intervene and mend the relationship. You can pray to God to send an angel to help your relationship. Assigned to your case will be the right angel or spirit guide. You may also call on Archangel Raguel who restores balance in relationships that are suddenly off kilter. He can mend any arguments or rifts that have risen. He will bring peace to all parties involved. Archangel Raguel is happy to do this for any type of connection, whether it is a love mate, friendship or colleague.

Chapter Seven

Stages Of Coupledom

Have you been in a situation where you are dating someone new and yet you have no idea what you are? By what you are, I mean are you dating, are you friends or are you in a relationship? What is the scenario? Many have professed uncertainty surrounding the appropriate title. They feel as if they are sitting in the dark not knowing what they are to the person whose company they enjoy. They might see the person they are dating as a good friendship, yet the connection feels like it is slightly more than a friendship. This will cause confusion and future pain if you are not talking about it.

You should never assume that you are together, but at the same time, your connection does need to be established. What if you are seeing someone who sees that you are both simply friends? You have wasted valuable time putting energy into a connection with someone who has no interest in a relationship. Another scenario would be that the other person feels you are in a relationship, and yet you do not. Therefore, you have been dating other people here and there while making a beeline to this other person who believes they are involved with you. This will also cause pain, heartache and damage to your connection. This kind of harm exists if one of you has more of an interest in your partnership and yet you carry on with it knowing this information. Edward was seeing Lisa regularly only to discover that there was never any clarity if they were together or not. They had been dating regularly for nearly a year at that point and had been intimate on top of that. Naturally, he assumed for that reason, that they were indeed an item. It turns out Lisa looked at the connection as if it were a friends with benefits union. She had been flirting with other people inappropriately outside of being with Edward.

The modern day world has come up with so many labels and tags to identify what people are that it feels like a buffet of noise. Labels are not important because two souls who operate on the same frequency know exactly what they are to one another. However, human souls feel more comfortable when they are able to identify what they are with this other person.

DATING

Dating is a word that has lost its meaning. The latest fad that seems to have taken a rise within the newer generations specifically is that they feel uncomfortable using the word, *'dating'*. Dating might mean that this is serious and I might have to commit. There is a ton of fear about merging with another soul. Merging with other souls is one of the main reasons you are here. It is an instinctive need to connect with someone else. Instead of using the word dating, there are great amounts of people who use the phrase, *'hanging out.'* Using the phrase, '*hanging out*', can and will cause confusion in a partnership that has not established what they are to begin with.

Dating is the process of getting to know someone gradually to see if you are a relationship match. You are not getting married or entering a serious relationship with them. However, dating is what leads to the more serious titles. Some couples may date for a month and part their separate ways, while others may date for years. If you are 'hanging out' with this person, going to restaurants, doing things together and kissing and being intimate on any level, then you are dating. There is no way to run from that title. This is the definition of what dating is.

Those who use the phrase, 'hanging out', tend to bypass the essential dating stages. Instead, they rush into a relationship with someone else within a month of knowing them. This is not a relationship just because you change your social networking status to 'in a relationship'. You cannot define a real relationship as such in less than three months. Those that do so will find that the dating connection has ended sooner than when you began it. You should be dating for several months getting to know that person over time. This is where you discover their interests and what they are like. You are looking to see if this is someone that you could see yourself going the distance with in a real relationship for decades to come. Take it seriously and treat it with the utmost care. Having a blasé attitude about dating means you are not ready to merge into a serious connection with anyone. It is also giving you a clue that the outcome will be failure.

How far into your hanging out before you bring up the inevitable question about what you both are? What if you bring it up too soon and scare the other person away? One would hope that common sense would be evident that you are dating regardless. The rules that modern day society has made in terms of what you are, has left most people living in a fog.

If you are hanging out with another human soul regularly, being intimate, or the attraction is there on both ends, then you should refrain from hanging out with other people beyond a friendship. Unfortunately, not everyone observes that rule. The media, peers and society have decided to make up their own rules. This has contributed to chaotic confusion with love and relationships. Human souls have free will choice to do as they please. As creative as the numerous rules may be, unfortunately they do not ensure longevity for a long-term relationship. Nor do they teach a soul about unconditional love or working with another soul. Someone will feel left out or unsure. One or both parties will sabotage the connection at some point. Poor choices lead to a buildup of Karma on your life path. You need to have the talk and do it soon before it gets out of hand.

It was not this complicated before the 1970's and 1980's. This was before free love and the sexual revolution, which brought in its plusses and negatives in the process. Everyone grew to be free in a way that the courting process became too complex, dynamic and therefore much more chaotic. It was the end of long-term committed relationships as ego modernized souls would come to know it. Before that time, two souls would endure a lengthy courting process, which involved a form of hanging out. They felt and observed the sexual tension even if they had not kissed yet. You did not go out searching, chatting and hanging out with other potentials while courting someone. Doing so is bad form and having no integrity. This is what shows you someone's character.

The Internet and phone apps that exist today connect everyone together, but they have also caused the relationship downfall. Technology did not shatter how relationships develop. It is the human ego, which has destroyed it. You give a child a new toy they are not ready to play with and you will have a problem. There are many who do not know how to properly court and date. Raised in a generation of texting, social networking, emailing, and phone apps have not helped with this. The ego wants more! It wants more friends, more people, more newness, more possibilities, more stimulation, more everything! The incessant search for immediate, self-gratifying, self-sabotaging sensations is a sign of detachment from your higher self, soul and God.

CASUALLY DATING VS. EXCLUSIVELY DATING

Define what you are together and agree on it. If you do not agree on it and neither of you is compromising, then you will run into issues.

Are you both going to agree that you are *Casually Dating* or are you *Exclusively Dating*?

Casually Dating means that you enjoy each other, but you are not serious or looking for anything serious. This is more or less someone you enjoy hanging out with. If either of you decided to stop it tomorrow, neither of you would care all that much. You may also be dating each other while dating other people casually as well. Of course, it is important that you are both on the same page that this is the set up you agreed on. Casually dating someone can be similar to a serial dater. This is someone who is always dating someone for a brief stint and then abruptly moves onto the next new person that enters their life. They are in love with the newness of someone. There are no hassles, no commitments and no responsibility needed. They are also chasing their tails. They may be dating several people at the same time or their dating scenarios with one person at a time are typically short-lived. They may also be the same people who add *'in a relationship'* to their social networking page status, even though they have just started dating that person. Within one to three months max they end up changing their social networking status back to *'single'*! They were never truly in a relationship to begin with. What they were doing was dating. They were never quite able to bring their dating situation to a REAL relationship efficiently. This is typically common with people younger than twenty-five who are inexperienced and tend to jump in immediately eliminating any essential courting process. It is not limited to someone under twenty-five as there are cases where people who are older do it as well. It is lacking in experience or having a deepened maturity level. This is a red flag, unless it is a scenario mutually agreed upon.

Exclusively Dating is where you are both loyal to one another through the dating process. You are incredibly interested in one another and you both want to see where it goes. You both imagined that you could be with this other person for life in a relationship. You are not dating around, seeing other people, or even chatting inappropriately with other people. You are investing time, energy and love into this person.

Dating can be tricky, because you do not immediately slap on the exclusively dating label, but it does happen fairly soon after a couple of months. You always start out with them as casually dating, but then as it continues to grow you are exclusively dating. You need to make sure that the other person is on the same page as you. This is the stage where you both may telepathically know you are an item, but you still have to clarify it. This should be easy for both as you are likely sharing much with one another to begin with. Exclusively dating one person is often termed also when the couple is not quite thinking of a serious relationship, even though they are seriously dating. The 'exclusive' terminology ensures that the couple knows they are devoted to one another only. The connection is a deep friendship, with some intimacy and the occasional date night. It might not be a full-fledged relationship, but to a degree, it is a relationship.

BOYFRIEND OR GIRLFRIEND

Some people are uncomfortable with the title of boyfriend or girlfriend. They are usually the same folks who do not use the dating word. Some acknowledgement of how you plan to refer to yourselves is helpful. Casually dating someone does not mean you are necessarily the boyfriend or girlfriend. If you are exclusively dating someone however, then you are a boyfriend or girlfriend.

Clarify this title with one another to make sure there are no surprises. There are many who are unsure what their connection is. Therefore, they continue dating other people or chatting them up. When people are hitting on you or asking you out, your immediate response should be, *"Thank you, but I'm seeing someone. I have a (boyfriend), (girlfriend)."*

RELATIONSHIP

A relationship is where you are committed to the person you have been exclusively dating for some time. Exclusively dating someone is a commitment, but a relationship is taking it to a higher level. You might still be using the boyfriend or girlfriend title on occasion, but you are in a full-fledged relationship as well. This means you have both acknowledged that you are in a relationship with one another. You have gone through the dating process with them and have come to the realization that this is someone you trust, love and want to share your life with at this point. This is not to say that you are not experiencing those feelings when you are exclusively dating someone, but a relationship is an entirely different ballgame. It is a beautiful moment and yet at the same time, it will take work to keep it afloat. The Romance Angels know that the work has only just begun when a real relationship starts. They are present for those who request their assistance while in a relationship. In a sense, it is like buying a house to a degree. You have to take care of that house, work on it, and keep it up. The same goes for your relationship.

A couple who is mature and responsible about forging on in a relationship knows the value and benefit of coming together in an even more committed way. They understand that it is a perfected dance. You understand each other's quirks and know how they operate.

If you do not communicate, then your relationship will disintegrate. This means opening up and discussing everything including the serious matters. You are partners and a team who have made a pact to forge on in life fighting the same cause together. You work through difficulties the way you might work with someone at your job in finding a solution to issues that arise. It is to know that you will have to compromise especially when your ego wants to do what it wants YOU to do. This is not living in the Light, but in selfishness. When you are selfish, self-centered and act out in your own interests, then you create bad Karma. This Karma grows when the particular choices you make negatively affect another human soul. This can include leaving a relationship to feed your ego. It is different when you leave an abusive relationship or that person has been engaging in intimate acts with other people. Even talking intimately with another person while you are involved with someone else is an emotional betrayal.

You might be riding sky high after you make a

selfish move that affects the one you left, but the initial selfish act you participated in grows and suddenly things start going wrong in your life. Most human souls do not realize that it is their Karma. When you are selfish, how would you know you acted selfishly? You are too self absorbed and narcissistic to care. Human souls have relationships throughout the course of their Earthly life in order to gain specific knowledge pertaining to their soul's agreement. No one is exempt from this regardless if one does not have at least one serious relationship in their life.

In a serious relationship, the couple usually tends to have their eye on living together at some point. There are many successful relationships where the couple has separate residences. In those cases, they are spending quite a bit of time practically living at each other's places. They might as well live together.

Relationships can also be anyone that your soul connects with for any length of time. This can be for a few minutes or a few decades. It can be your love relationship mate, your boss, colleague, a friend or even neighbor. It can be someone you have met in an airport terminal holed up together for a two-hour delay. You share a conversation that enlightens or prompts you to make a positive change within you. They might have connected with you to deliver specific information that ends up assisting you with something more pressing in your life.

When you merge into an actual love relationship, you have likely experienced some ups and downs with that person during the dating stages. You know how to navigate effectively with each other when there is a disagreement. When you were exclusively dating, you might not have shared every moment or your whereabouts, however in a relationship, it is a mutual alliance. You will be receiving questions that you might not have had before. "I saw you talking to that girl. What was that about?" How about, "Can you accompany me to this work thing?"

In a relationship, you are already aware that your mate may need extra reassurance that you are with them from time to time. You know how your mate is and will not be exactly like you. Perhaps they need additional emotional support or physical affection. Maybe they crave heavy doses of romance or they prefer not to have the hearts and flowers kind of love. These are situations where the couple does these things for their partner, because they care about them. It might not be what they are typically into, but this is where compromise comes into play. You gain knowledge in the relationship such as opening up or revealing your heart more. You are here on this planet for love after all. Do you really think it's to work a 9-6 job for the duration of your Earth life? Sure, you need to make money to survive, but that's not why you are here. It is to learn to love and exude love.

It is awesome to be an enterprising person in business, and to strive for financial success that ensures the stability and security your human needs crave. However, you do not want it to take over your life to the point where you ignore your mate indefinitely. There will be times where you might have a busy period at work. It is another thing to allow it to consume and rule your entire Earthly life. The Romance Angels stress on the need for you to balance both your work and your home life. Doing this ensures that you are in a happier state of mind while attracting in the abundance your human soul desires.

By the time you are in a relationship with this person, you already know them pretty well. This means you know what some of their faults and moods are like. You know how they are, what makes them tick, or what upsets them. You need to be at a place of being open with that other person when you cross over into the 'in a relationship' territory. At that point, you may have already discussed if you will one day live together and what kind of places or cities you would like to live in. You discover if it is in harmony with the other person during the dating phase. You know if they want kids, or a family, or pets, etc.

How is your partner with children, animals or their own family? These are clues to what they might be like when you are living with them. When you are living with someone in a relationship, you are with this person day in and day out. Is this something your ego will be able to handle? It is certainly important that the partnership have their separate lives and hobbies to an extent. If you are with the same person every second, then you will be driven crazy. Human souls need space and independence every now and then. This helps them realign and reassess their goals, visions and thoughts. Successful couples are in constant communication with one another even if they are on a sabbatical alone while the other is teaching a class in another city. Many households have couples where both of them work all day. When they arrive at home at the end of the day, they may have personal activities to attend to. Maybe one of them enjoys swimming at the gym after work on Wednesday's while another meets his buddies on the field for a baseball sport. Healthy relationships welcome the separate, but equal lives they have together. This ensures the longevity while keeping it all balanced.

You are each other's friend and confidante. Having your own life is beneficial pending that you do not neglect your partner. Some long-term successful couples have protested that the passion or the sex has waned at times while together. Passion and sex in a relationship is a helpful component, but it is normal for happy committed couples to reach a place of no sex or a drought. When this happens, you must talk about it with one another. Take it seriously by finding ways to unleash the passions within you both. This should not be too difficult because all of the other positive components that keep you together already exist. This is why you are together to begin with. When you have the other positive qualities in the relationship such as a great friendship, companionship, communication, trust and enjoyment together, then it is relatively easy to move it into a sexual way.

Growing subconscious fears contribute to lack

of sex in a relationship. Some couples become too comfortable with each other where it feels like you are roommates or siblings. This does not mean your relationship is over. On the contrary, this is where you put those working on the relationship skills to good use. Find ways to re-ignite that exciting passion between you both. I have a strong sexual drive by nature, but I am also very patient with someone I love when it comes to that. You may need to put in some effort and not be afraid to talk sexually with your partner. Send them little sexual texts and emails or start complimenting them and their body. Your partner should be open and receptive to this. Drop your guard and those pointless walls built around you and let loose with each other. Come up with some sexual exercises that you can both work on together. Develop self-love for your own body and your lovers' body. If you do not love yourself, then how can you love someone else? Take romantic trips with one another and put together candle light dinners. Hold hands more. Cuddle. Hug. Get into it and put in some effort!

You should never jump to move in with someone in a relationship right away. Wait until the honeymoon blush has worn off. This is about the 18-month mark after you first met or started dating. If they have lasted that long with you, then you know there is a great shot at making the living together part work. There is no set time on when you have to move in, as there are couples that have been in relationships with each other for years, but choose not to live together nor have immediate plans to. Exceptions always exist such as an older couple who comes together and gets married within the same year. They have the maturity level to ensure it lasts. They don't have the excessive hang ups that come with someone who is younger.

There is no such thing as an open relationship despite the modern day world pushing for that title. Open relationships are essentially, *'friends with benefits'*. This is what it should be labeled. There are swinger couples that live with one person in a relationship, but might be unsatisfied sexually with that person. They prefer to invite another person into the bedroom on occasion. They are more into sex and agree on living together for companionship, while bringing in additional partners for sexual enjoyment. This is a mutually reciprocated agreement between them.

MARRIAGE, CIVIL UNION, COMMITMENT

Marriage, civil union, or a commitment ceremony is the next step after relationship. You have been in a relationship with the same person for years and you are both happy with it. You may both choose to make it even more official. This is where you are taking a big step in joining in a marriage under the eyes of human law. This includes all the tax benefits that it entails. This also includes the dangers if you decide to divorce. It can be taxing financially and emotionally if you are both not in sync when you decide to dissolve the marriage. Marriage is not always a romantic circumstance, although it can be. It is a business alliance as if you are starting your own business with a partner. This partner is your soul mate and they are on the same page with you. You both already know quite a bit about the other person and you function well as a team. You are each other's family through all good things and bad. Only marry when you have no problem knowing there is no out. You know there will be lows as well as great highs and you are still okay with that. You will work together to fix it as if it were your business. You would not walk away from your business immediately if there were problems, would you? You would find ways to fix it.

Another label for marriage can be a civil union or some choose to conduct an official ceremony even if the government does not recognize it. This might be the case with Same Sex couples in certain states or countries. The bottom line is that it does not matter what the law, government or other people think about your relationship. It only matters what you and your partner choose to call it. You may choose to say you are married, even if you did not go to a government facility to have it documented under the eyes of the law. Some couples like to have a special spiritual ceremony whether it is personal between them, or an all out wedding with all the trimmings and guests. This is in keeping with the fun and joy that a love relationship is. Love is a celebration!

A Quick Word

A great deal of human souls are struggling or suffering in relationship connections today. Due to the abundant amount of similar troubles and questions others have regarding love and relationships, I've included additional information and guidance surrounding those concerns in this book. In the following chapters 6-9 we will cover and discuss some of the bleaker issues related to love connections with soul mates in this modern day world. This is content taken from the big *Warrior of Light* book, *Darkness of Ego*.

Chapter Eight

The Ego's War On Love

Human souls crave contact and love from others, even if the hardened ego denies it. Those who prefer to be loners, independent or living in the middle of the woods with no one else around grew to be this way due to societal conditioning during their younger life's developmental years. Deep within the DNA of the soul's core, the soul desires a love companion. This is the case even if the love companion they crave is independent natured themselves. An independent minded loner would have a better chance of going the distance with someone who is similar in that respect. You do your thing, I'll do mine, and every now and then we do our thing together.

One might not call this a love companion, but a friend companion. It's still a love companion regardless of the title you give it. The nature of closeness you have with this person is irrelevant.

Your one true long term soul mate this lifetime could be the same gender as you. You might be sexually attracted to someone of the opposite sex, and yet the love companion you choose to be around through the duration of your current Earthly life is of the same sex. This doesn't have anything to do with engaging in physical intimacy with this person. There are a great deal of love relationships between two people where they are with someone of the same gender, but do not engage in physical intimacy because sexually they're attracted to someone of the opposite sex. This is the same case with someone who might be attracted to the same sex, but their soul mate lifetime love is someone of the opposite sex. These cases are just as much a deeper higher love than any other physical relationship. This is someone you feel the most comfortable spending the rest of your current Earthly life with. Over time you come to the conclusion that the person you want to be with is this particular person.

Some might flinch confused believing that the one true soul mate intended for them is supposed to be someone they have a sexually, passionate, hot love relationship with. Yes, this soul mate can have those qualities with you, but this isn't always the case for many souls on Earth.

One of the bigger misconceptions about long term love relationships is that human souls have this misunderstood belief that if there is no sex with a love partner, then the relationship must be over or they're not with the right one. The angels say this myth couldn't be further from the truth in real reality. It is the ego demanding that relationships satisfy their insatiable needs. There is a great deal of soul mate love relationships where they experience a sexual drought. It feels as if they're stuck in a rut and have become more like roommates or siblings. There is a block that prevents them from being able to adequately move into a regular sexual physical relationship with one another. This can be shifted when both partners discuss this issue openly and with compassion. They both agree to take steps and make effort to be more physically intimate with one another. This is in order for the partnership to thrive and grow. Your higher self's soul is open in all ways conceivable. This goes for physical intimacy with a love partner too!

The other case is there is no physical sexual intimacy with the soul mate if it's a love connection with a friend who is of a gender you're not sexually attracted to in your lifetime. In this sexually charged world, this is a difficult concept for modern day human souls to comprehend, but Earthly life is slow to evolve to a higher space where complex circumstances unseen are understood.

The ability to love, give love, and receive love are part of every soul's make up when it enters into an Earthly life. Human souls were not born unfriendly, greedy, angry and selfish. This is the human ego and lower self running the show. It is not ones higher self, which is pure love and compassion. When someone displays love, joy and compassion traits all at once without wanting anything in return, then you can be sure that at that moment they're operating from their higher self's space. You've likely encountered this type of person in your life that exudes those traits. They are infectious and brighten your world just by being in your vicinity. Wouldn't you rather be in that space full time, rather than in upset and stress?

It is understood that you live in a world with tampering energies around you. If you live in a big, unfriendly city, then you likely know how difficult it can be to navigate through the tempestuous waters day after day with angry, rushed souls around you. The love is nowhere to be found and you feel this, but often so does the angry soul. They've hardened becoming jaded and unlovable to themselves and other human souls. Yet, deep down at their soul's core resides the love they were born with. Their ego has rendered it inaccessible caging it and sealing in the goodness. This is why there are souls experiencing an Earthly life for the specific purposes of awakening and opening the hearts of these hardened souls. They might be someone the hardened soul crosses paths with and is showered with love and kindness from this other soul in passing. It allows a few cracks of light to burst out of the hardened soul's heart chakra.

It takes work to reach a state of serenity. Sometimes you will falter and lose your way. All souls are works in progress. This includes the teachers and leaders of the world. When you gain the tools necessary to pull yourself out of the ugliness, then it gets easier to do so in those moments when you waver.

Love relationships in modern day era have grown to become more than an effort to find and a struggle to keep. Since many human souls are governed ruthlessly by the external and the ego, this has played a huge part in the demise of loving relationships. In the United States alone, polls and stats are being revealed that slightly more than half of the population consider themselves to be single. This data isn't taken seriously by anyone, and neither is the tragic reality pointed out. This is a sad revelation that further demonstrates that humanity is not evolving as quickly as one would like to believe. It is ironic considering that love is the reason all souls are here. Obsessions center on needs, excess, and selfish satisfaction. This satiating need to sharpen in on external fixation was taught to others by the masses in the media, your peers and society. This progression continues to be recycled generation after generation. It's a strange kind of zombie like transfixed eeriness that hones in on all things greed, material or external. Some human souls attempt to receive this need for love through external sources such as social media adoration. This is not love, but ego. It is done innocently at times since this is a soul who simply craves love.

It is easy to hypnotize a baby soul more than any other. Baby souls are on Earth for their first Earthly life run. The angels see them as naïve and innocent. Other spirits see them as dangerous, causing the most hate, destruction, issues and drama around the world. The baby souls are all of those things combined. They are both naïve and destructive. They're easily influenced and succumb to the intoxication of the images being fed to them. This is done instead of diving deeper into pulling out their true higher self's soul. If this isn't the case, then the soul is terribly unhappy with some part of their life. They might be under stress and experiencing prolonged feelings of negativity.

Social media and phone apps have also contributed to the downfall of long term relationships. There are positive benefits to social media, but what are the benefits with phone apps? The lonely and bored typically log on to connect with preying predators looking for the next best thing, or to fill up the emptiness the ego created within. You are one in a long line of people that someone is sending the same messages to. The rise in phone apps to meet people is another avenue to come into contact with those in your vicinity. This has its benefits to a degree for those who are either temporarily single, living in a small town with little to no people, or for hooking up. This can be misconstrued as a broad generalization, but we're not speaking in specifics.

Through research, I've discovered most people ultimately use dating apps for the means of hooking up with you at some point. Phone apps are a way to meet people in your vicinity at the touch of your finger tips. This is an exciting and alluring way to hopefully meet additional people who you hope will become important in your life. The issue is that the ego is looking for instant gratification with many, instead of developing something meaningful and long lasting with one person. These avenues satisfy the ego, temporarily relieve boredom, and fulfill ravenous addictions.

Some of the common inquiries I receive from others are where they are dating someone new or already in a love relationship with them. It isn't long before they come to me with a discovery. They discover by "accident" that the person they're involved with is on a phone app. They express confusion and concern unsure whether or not to say something to their partner. They don't want to upset them or find out they're up to no good. Instead they hope they can trust their partner enough to assume they're just on the app for friends. Friends with a gender they are attracted to? Sure it's possible, but it would lead a rational soul to question it.

This further cements that most have already placed a negative stigma on the use of phone apps. There are good people wherever you go, including on a phone app. The flip side is that it can be a device for narcissism and addiction. You're logging on day after day hoping someone can fill the emptiness that resides within you. This soon lowers your vibration leaving you perpetually glum and dissatisfied. You're searching and searching for people to connect with on the app. What about the people you know in person? These are the ones who are already in your life. I've watched a great many throw that away only to log onto a phone dating app looking for new people to develop nothing with. It's a cycle that never ends.

Relationships are colder than they've ever been in this modern day, yet somewhat backwards civilization. The hyper-technological world has contributed heavily to the demise of real human connections. The irony is the issues going on in the world are stemming from disconnect with one's true soul and higher self.

Before the rise in social media and phone apps, human souls took the connections they had seriously. Now they disregard them on a whim for the next best thing that pops up on their phone. Operating from ego, boredom, or loneliness ultimately lowers your vibration. One is craving instant stimulation from anyone around them. It doesn't matter who it is. Most on phone apps are ultimately looking for a one night stand. Some will cut the foreplay and come right out and tell you, while others will work you a little bit before dropping the bomb that they're deeply and crazy attracted to you. You feel loved for a brief moment that someone finds your photo or photos attractive. Eventually your banter between one another dissolves as this person has moved onto someone else they're chatting with and saying the same remote things to. It's a cycle that repeats itself as you log back on and continue this drill with the next victim wondering if any of these people could be 'the one'. If they're not attracted to you, it's rare that they would attempt to get to know you at all. Everything is externally based. Do I like how you appear before I engage with more than a hello?

Your soul longs for the kind of eternal gratifying stimulation that cannot be fulfilled through immediate indulgence. It's an addiction within the ego that one feeds in hopes of finding the one awesome love, friend, or one night stand. This tears down your soul thus lowering your vibration in the process. It's the search that crushes your soul.

I've reviewed many cases where love relationships fell apart. Both partners end up back on social media and the apps searching instead of working on the connection they had. One or both will say something like, "Well our relationship was great, but there was something missing." They'll make a variety of excuses that are fixable in the eyes of someone operating from their higher self. There is no perfect relationship and it will always seem as if something is missing no matter who you are with. This is how you learn important soul enhancing traits while with someone. You accept your partner's neurosis as they do with you.

The ego is strong in others and demands to have all of its needs met at once. This is a false reality that will leave the human soul perpetually dissatisfied. As you grow older and find yourself alone feeling even more abandoned, your mind sifts through the many options and choices of soul mates that entered your vicinity during the course of your life. There may be one soul mate in particular that your mind drifts over to from time to time. You'll wish you could do things differently with them, such as make it work and not throw in the towel. Human souls are intended to partner up with one another in soul mate relationships and companionships. This strengthens your souls by merging both your lights. You have that loving, supportive companionship through all of your years on Earth. You are the anchor for each other when things get tough. It helps to have that other half to make decisions with while granting them and yourself the space your soul also requires for clarity. When you partner with the right soul mate relationship dynamic, then you add balance to your life that keeps you from diving too far off into the deep end.

When you ultimately merge into a love relationship, then remember to love each other up often. Touch, hug, and cuddle with one another. The physical body hugging another physical body adds positive health benefits. Clairvoyantly one might see the aura light around both people hugging. The light in both souls merges and the colors of their aura shifts from a dark muddy color if they were stressed to brightening up. This is doubling the power and effects that the hug has. It releases Oxytocin in the brain and relaxes the soul. Tests have been conducted on hugging where they measure the blood pressure in someone who is stressed out. The blood pressure rises in the soul who is lacking of hugs. While the one receiving or giving a hug displays a drop in blood pressure preceding a stress event. Hug someone whenever you can and spread the love. You can hug a friend, a tree, and even animals. Although the hug of a love interest has a massive health benefit due to the high passion and love quotient between them.

Chapter Nine

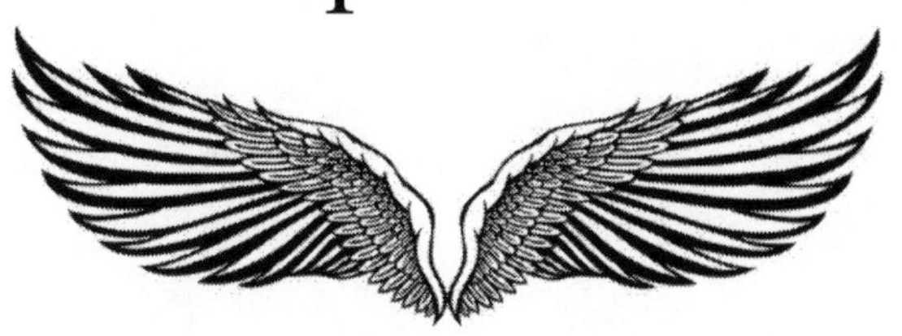

Bring Back My Lover

Love issues are more frequent than ever before due to the heavy rule of ego in this materialistic externally based world. One of the biggest inquiries I receive surrounding love is that someone's lover abruptly leaves the relationship. This results in the one who was left to feel eternally dejected. The partner that was left desires heavenly intervention to bring them back together again. Heaven cannot force someone to act a certain way against their will. For some cases, they might plant the idea in that person's mind only if it will benefit both of the souls higher good. And if it is part of the agreement both soul's made prior to entering an Earthly life. There may be cases where you believe with all your heart that your relationship ended prematurely. This may be the case to your ego, but not to your ex-partner or your Guides and Angels.

Not all relationship connections are intended to last forever. It is not uncommon to have strong feelings for your partner after they've exited the relationship. Your mind goes through a whirlwind of feelings that include sadness, anger, and pride rejection. You miss the good times you had and love the security that the connection provided. You're left in a state of shock mulling it over in your mind repeatedly trying to understand how the breakup could happen. This causes confusion as you thought everything was fine in the relationship.

You reach out to anyone who will listen to your troubles surrounding it. This is with the hope that this person you're reaching out to will offer you answers that will bring your lover back to you. This can be from friends, strangers, colleagues, therapists to psychic readers. Inside you desire that they will all tell you that this is just a temporary break and you'll be back together before you know it. In some cases, this does happen of course, but not always.

I've been in those love connections in the past where it was bliss without any major issues or arguments and it ended only to be rekindled again years later. I've also witnessed the red flags in other people's relationship connections, which both partners were blind to seeing. The person who was left in a relationship is in a state of shock. They are unable to admit the red flags were indeed present if they examine the connection trajectory more closely. You ignore the red flags when you're in love. If you notice the red flags, you think the person will change only to later discover they've ultimately left you in turmoil and heartache.

If you were left in a relationship by someone you deeply loved, then request heavenly assistance from your Spirit team. Ask that they help re-kindle the spark lost between you and your ex mate. If your Spirit team sees that the relationship is indeed over and has run its course, then add that they help you heal and move on. If they intervene to assist your lover to come back to you, this doesn't mean that person will acknowledge the heavenly guidance and nudges. Many do not listen to their Guides and Angels due to the over consumption of the ego and material world around them. The exception is a spiritually minded partner, but a spiritually minded partner likely would not have left their mate in the first place unless they were abusive in some form or bathed in addictions. Another exception is that the partner is moving into a period of soul searching and discovering who they are. They require space for a major transition. However, a spiritually minded partner more than likely would've discussed the break up with you so that you are both at peace with the splitting up.

The soul mate you love has left you and chosen to pull away. They distanced themselves from your connection for a myriad of reasons. You anxiously wonder and obsess if your lover will come back to you. You believe you received signs that they're interested in you regardless that they left. The angels know if a couple has what it takes to re-unite and make it work, but they cannot intervene with the other person's free will. If someone bailed out of the relationship, they do so out of free will and ego. This is powerful beyond any kind of heavenly intervention. It is important to note this since I have had others say they've asked Heaven or their Guides for help in re-uniting them with their ex in a love relationship, yet months have passed by and there has been no movement or sign of it happening.

Heaven does not have control over how someone chooses to respond or not respond to your affections. The person you desire will show how they feel about you through their actions. Believe them when they show this. They might be unresponsive to your affections after the break up. When someone is interested, they will let it be known. When you reach out to someone you have interest in to see if they have interest in you, then do it with the knowledge they might not give you the response you crave, if any response at all. Prepare yourself for this and accept any outcome. This person made a decision to extricate themselves from your connection. This doesn't necessarily mean you did anything to cause that, which is something else that may plague your thoughts. You're likely to go through deep self-analysis to see where you might have played a part in the crumbling of the union. Sometimes you'll see where you made mistakes. Other times the breakup doesn't have anything to do with what you or they did or did not do.

Friends may urge you to move on and immediately see other people. Feel whole and complete within before you venture out into the dating field. This is another side effect after someone has left you in a relationship. You understandably want to get over it and move on as quickly as possible. This isn't fair to someone new when you're not ready and still have deep thoughts lingering over your previous partner. Understand the lessons that have been learned in the connection that ended abruptly. If the connection was submerged in red flags, unhappiness, or abuse, then in the future make a pact to only accept soul mate relationships that are loving and supportive. These are ones that enrich and nourish you, while you give this same support in return. Refuse to be part of any drama with a soul mate that makes you feel less than others. Aim to be around people whose lives are working. Choose to be around those who are making positive contributions. Be around those who are growing, evolving, and making soul contact. Sometimes you need to release soul mates because they are harmful in toxic ways you might not have been noticing, either to themselves or towards you.

There will be times when your ego has a difficult time letting go of an ex. You have loving memories of the good times you had with them. The ego refuses to believe that the connection and lessons with them are over. You wait and hope for that small glimmer of hope that there will be some reuniting taking place one day. Meanwhile, years have passed and there's been no movement. What will it take to see that the connection is indeed over? Sure there are cases where there is a reuniting that takes place in order to complete unfinished business, but those are rare cases. Incidentally, I have personally had that happen where one of my soul mates and I re-united years later and moved into a love relationship. The relationship was stronger the second time around. Regardless, it is vital to move on and start living again. Get back into the joy of your life. If someone is meant to be with you including your ex, then the re-kindling will happen naturally on divine timing.

I never advise that someone wait for someone who left them, no matter how big the feelings are. An exception would be if you have both discussed that you're taking a break or one of you needs your space. If you wait around hopeful that your ex will return, then this can create a block from allowing someone new from coming in to an extent. It becomes difficult for a new person to enter the picture unless it is the lifelong marriage soul mate. A sensitive person or the kind of love mate you desire will sense an ex's energy around you even if they're not aware of it. It's in your aura. When you pine over someone no longer with you, then your body language may slump more than usual without knowing it. Your energy may be suppressed showing signs of a prolonged disappointment with something in your life. This energy you're giving off is not conducive to attracting in a new love partner. You have to move on with your life. If your ex comes back one day to mend your connection, then great! If not, at least you'll be living.

It saddens the angels to see so many struggling

in love relationships today. You were involved with someone romantically, only to have them pull out of your connection unexpectedly. One day everything seems like it was going great and the next day you get a message out of the blue that they lost interest. You wonder how it was easy for them to pull out or how they sleep at night. It's almost as if a light switch was turned off and they were no longer interested in a relationship with you. You were kind, compassionate, and loyal to this person. You attempt to make sense of it and wonder what you did wrong. You grow angry feeling like they wasted your time. You might find it difficult to pull through each day. Meanwhile, you know they've gone on and they're busy with their life as if what they did had zero effect on you.

If someone pulled out in this manner, it's likely they were already entertaining the idea of leaving you for some time, but putting on the face that all is well beforehand. If they were merely looking to pull out a month before they did out of the blue, then this is a behavioral pattern with them where they pull out of everything with a snap of a finger. It's not someone you would want to engage in a long term relationship with anyway. It is a form of deception and having deceptive energy in a relationship is not healthy for a long term relationship. You may have bit the bullet with this connection. Treasure the great time and experiences you had with your ex. Make your peace with it and let it go. This will lift your vibration which will help attract in someone awesome!

Chapter Ten

Getting Over An Ex Lover

You've come to the realization that your ex who left you has indeed moved on. It's been months or even longer and there has been zero communication. They've either moved away or ended up in a love relationship with someone else. You now know that it is over. Coming to this reality might be painful, but it is also freeing on your soul as well. When someone leaves you, then you do not need to go through it alone. You will be tempted to email, text, and call this person with upset emotions. Some do the 'drunk dial'. The guidance is that you leave it alone. Nine times out of ten when you do reach out to them upset it has a tendency to back fire or blow up in your face. You come at your ex with heavy emotion and distress. Your ex is turned off and repelled by this energy.

When you have no feelings for someone and they come at you with heavy emotions of anger and upset, the human instinct is to immediately display annoyance and anger. Although, if it's someone you truly love, then you want to talk it over with them. This is another clue that the person that left has lost interest at that time. Knowing this information is helpful as much as it feels like someone is killing you.

Write what you want to say to your ex-lover in an email or letter, but do not send it to them. Send it to yourself or a trusted friend who understands. Lashing out at the ex will not cause a dent except push them further away. They've already made the decision to walk away from you. They are not going to care much about how the split has upset you or what you have to say. They have absolved themselves of any responsibility with you.

I've received cases where someone wants to send their ex this letter. It should only be done when you know for sure that you are finished with them. Most of the time I've discovered that they're really only sending the letter in hopes of eliciting a positive response from their ex. Immediately the next day I will hear them say that there was no response to what they sent, or that it backfired with the ex telling them to leave them alone.

Why are you questioning that there is no response from your message to them? You sent the letter releasing the pain off your chest knowing that you're officially walking away. This letter does not contain anything positive, but is merely a recounting of all the times this ex hurt you. There is some colorful foul language sprinkled in it for good measure. Then they end the letter with, "If you still want to talk and work this out I'm available." This will not prompt the ex to grow a conscious.

You will need to work on getting through each day. Pre-occupy yourself with positive activities and healthy distractions as much as possible. Get to the space where you are feeling joy again. The depressing feelings surrounding your ex will be less hurtful as time progresses. It will be difficult at first as you push yourself to go to the gym when it's typically an easy occurrence for you. You just want to stay in bed or lie on the floor and not move. You grin and bear it. You pray and ask for heavenly assistance everyday and you keep going.

Let go of the why's, how's, and I don't understands. Make your peace with the connection dissolving. There will be no way to wrap your mind around it no matter how you look at it and dissect it to death. You have to allow yourself to move through each of the stages of emotions such as sadness, depression, then anger and resentment. Eventually this is followed by a transformation where you reach a place of peace and forgiveness for yourself and for your ex love. This is where you accept that this is the path your ex chose and you respect that. You do not need to take any responsibility for their actions. Thank them for the time you had together. Forgive them for your soul's benefit and then let the energy surrounding them go. There is no timeline for these emotions to work themselves out, but reaching the place where you're completely content again is the goal. It is where you can think of them and it is no longer painful. You discover they're with someone new and that does not bother you. Any difficult emotions experienced do more damage to you than anyone else. No one is worth that kind of pain.

Avoid remaining in contact with your ex when possible. When you have heightened love feelings for your ex and you were the one who was left, then this can be taxing on your psyche. You never truly move through the various stages of emotions in order to start living again. You find you're getting used to moving on in life without them, then suddenly they surface with a text hello and you're right back where you started. The love feelings come up again. You grow hopeful that perhaps because they're remaining in touch there is a possibility of rekindling the love connection. Whenever your ex reaches out to you it prolongs the pain. You'll be afraid to let them go and avoid contact because you do love them. However, know that constantly engaging with them when you have deep feelings for them can confuse you into believing there is still hope with them. That is until you discover they have added the *'in a relationship'* with someone else status on their social media account.

When experiencing heartache over a love interest leaving you, then call upon Archangel Raphael and Archangel Azrael. Ask to be infused with healing love energy daily until you discover you've indeed moved on. The thoughts of your ex no longer bring you any pain or emotional discomfort. This means that you are no longer affected by posts they put up on social media, or when you receive that random text hello from them. You'll know when it's safe to form a friendship with your ex if this is what you both choose. It'll be the moment where your ex is with a new love interest and that does not bother you on any negative level.

When praying and asking for help, understand that sometimes your Spirit team will not always bring you what you want if they feel it is not going to benefit your higher self in the long run. They know what's to come up ahead and what you must endure. You might profusely request help and ask that a particular soul mate contacts you, but it does not come to fruition. There are a couple of factors that would prevent that from happening. The ex's free will choice. Consider also that your Spirit team is blocking it from happening at that time for your own soul's benefit. The answers as to when it will happen cannot be understood until time has passed. This is when all will be revealed.

Ask yourself the serious questions as to how you wish to proceed from this point on. Soul mates come and go in your life. Not all soul mates are intended to stay no matter how much of a huge impact they've had on you. Ask yourself the tough questions such as: "Is the soul work with my ex indeed done? If so, how long will I allow this breakup prevent me from moving forward?"

It's not uncommon for some human souls to have that great love they will never forget. For some it can be their first love. It can be the one they had when they were younger before they grew older and became more jaded to love. Perhaps it happened later in life. Fear keeps people in relationships that are long over. They're too comfortable and afraid to make a drastic change by walking away from a connection they've been unhappy in for years. Change is disruptive to human souls. If you do not change toxic situations, then you'll remain miserable!

It can be difficult for some souls to emotionally detach from someone they were intimate with for a long period of time. Most human souls do not automatically switch to being friends after a serious love relationship ends. The brief connections they had which only lasted a month or two can merge into a friendship with no problem. This is because you're not emotionally attached to them. The long term relationships are another story where there was a stronger long term bond. If you have deep emotions over a love connection that only lasted one to three months, then take caution with future love potentials. Avoid wearing your heart on your sleeve so soon with someone you do not know.

Having to put on the face day after day is exhausting as you attempt to get over an ex. You still have to go to work or the grocery store. You're inevitably going to see and bump into people depending on where you live. It is okay to give yourself permission to not engage with anybody unless necessary. The hurt and pain will come and go. Sometimes you'll be fine and other times you won't be, but over time it will diminish. Just keep moving forward and take it day to day. It's normal to have confused emotional reactions to someone else's behavior following a breakup.

Those who pull out of a love connection with someone they love might be seen as being in a state of self-centeredness, or going through a selfish period. Sometimes this is the case, but other times it's not. It's easy for the ego to grow angry when a lover leaves them. It's important to also consider that this ex-lover discovered while in a relationship with you that it is not what they desire. They might long to be free and thought they could do the 'relationship thing', only to discover it's not for them. Or perhaps they have some soul searching to do that requires they leave the relationship. Everyone is on their own soul path. It's crucial to step away from the tantrums of your ego and respect that.

There are souls who indeed have a pattern of using others in a love relationship. They might be the ones who do not have a history of successful long term relationships. They have a history of being in short lived connections only to grow bored and leave most of them sooner than later. They are living in the moment and thinking of themselves. They are not in touch with how their actions might affect someone else. If they do know and do not care, then that would make them a sociopath. Sociopaths do not have deep emotions for others. Selfish would be a more appropriate word. Selfish people do not change overnight. Learning to be selfless takes quite a bit of time. The selfish individual needs to want to become more selfless, but it's difficult for their ego to convince them that this is what indeed needs to happen. The selfish person is not out to get you, but are thinking of themselves first. This becomes a bigger problem when it negatively affects those around the selfish person. The selfish person is too selfish to notice that their behavior is affecting others around them. Never wait for a selfish person to suddenly grow a conscious if it's never been part of their nature. In hindsight, if you examined the red flags in this type of connection, then you might see the signs that your connection would not last to begin with. You likely brushed it off until this person really did something awful to your heart.

While in the dating process, pre-screen your potential soul mates entering the picture. This way you can get a feel for the kinds of relationships this person has been in and what they desire in a love relationship. Dates that are serious about you tend to ask: "How long was your longest relationship?" If the answer is three months, well, I think you have your probable answer as to how it's likely going to go. When your love relationship ends, remain strong and pre-occupy yourself with fun activities, even if you have moments where tears form. Do not put too much pressure on your soul. You deserve respect from those you have shown love to.

Nothing is ever final even if it feels that way. Your ego wants to convince you that the despair is real. It is real in the way that your human soul knows it to be real in the physical world, but it's not real in the grand long term sense. Allow your soul to breathe by moving swiftly through the traumatic experience. Moments of hurt will twinge your side from time to time. You might mask that with an addiction. While other times you'll push yourself to go to the gym. I've felt this kind of pain when it comes to a deep, loving relationship split. In my previous life, I found that I had a habit of attracting in soul mates that were living in the moment. They love you today, but tomorrow they likely will not. This is giving your power away to someone you put faith into. You realize they are flawed and have issues as we all do, but the issues they wrestle with have nothing to do with you. Unfortunately, sometimes it is at the expense of others. Everyone's lives are constantly changing and altering. Nothing stays the same even if one wanted it to. The ending of a deep love relationship feels like a death. Your views and life take on an entirely new turn. Someone loses their job they thought they would be at forever. Their life is altered by that one act. They have to make plans they otherwise would not have.

Perhaps months have passed and you're still battling cutting the cords with your ex. If you believe your connection with them is worth saving, then reach out for one last bit of hope. The odds of them coming around and initiating a move could be slim. At least if time has passed, the heated emotions might have subsided with you and your ex. You might be able to communicate peacefully. If you do reach out to them, do it knowing that you might not get the response you're hoping for or they might not have any romantic interest in you. However, you will have your definite answer depending on the way your ex has responded. This can give you peace of mind that it may be time to cut the cords from the attachment to this soul mate for good. This way you are not stalling your soul from experiencing prosperous new connections. If your energy is heavily invested in this ex soul mate, then this can deter a new suitor who is trying to enter the picture. Someone who is high vibrational can sense an ex energy in someone.

A relationship break up puts you at a cross roads in attempting to forge on with or without them. You come to the realization that you need to make a choice. Will you hang on to your ex's essence in the hopes that there is still that possibility? Or will you open the door a crack for someone amazing and more aligned with you to enter the picture? This would be someone new who genuinely has an attraction and feelings for you. They're facing the same direction as you and value long term committed relationships. Even if you do move forward, it does not mean that this ex soul mate and you cannot become a romantic item at a later date, but until then at least you'll be out there living!

Chapter Eleven

Soul Connections

If the important love relationship soul mate is to enter the picture for someone, then nothing is going to stop that person from connecting with you. This includes free will choice. Free will choice can delay the connection from happening, but it will not delay it forever. Your guides and angels team up with your soul mate's guides and angels to orchestrate the connection. Once the connection is made, there is little that can stop it from moving forward. You both immediately take notice. Anything that does stop it from moving forward is temporary. Sometimes how it happens is that you continue to bump into this person until you both finally lock eyes. From that point, nothing stops you from communicating. You both know this is it. Note we said if it is the big soul mate that is intended to be the life partner mate. There is a synchronicity set up taking place in order to bring two souls together.

Everyone has numerous soul mates sifting in and out of their vicinity during the course of their lives. In this case, this is the love soul mate marriage that you connect with who sticks with you through the duration of your Earthly life in a love connection. These are not the soul mate relationships that come in the guises of friendships, colleagues or short lived love relationships. Those are soul mates as well who you made a previous agreement with. This is in order to connect to them briefly for a specific purpose. This can be such as balancing previous karma with that soul. They might be an awakener for you to prepare you for the REAL lifelong soul mate relationship.

If your soul is not ready for the real deal and you have additional tools to gain, then you will have a short lived soul mate enter the picture before the long term one comes in. You may even have many short lived soul mate relationships for a good chunk of your life before you are with the long term mate. If you are thrown to the wolves prematurely with the long term mate immediately, then it may end unhappily. You will both likely incarnate relatively at the same time repeatedly until the connection is balanced.

There is no stopping any soul mate connection from happening. If it's not happening with someone, then they are likely not the intended big relationship soul mate. You will know they are the lifelong mate, because you end up together for most or the rest of your current Earthly life.

Long Distance Relationships

There is a belief that one's soul mate might be living in another state or country. Your Spirit team would not place your lifelong soul mate somewhere else when you live thousands of miles away. If that were the case, it would be orchestrated or foreseen by your Spirit team that one or the both of you are going to eventually move to the same city, state or country you live in relatively soon. This would be within one to five years after the meeting or initial connection contact takes place.

There are many cases where lifelong soul mates and especially twin flames have crossed paths with one another while not living in the same state or country. This is more common with the twin flame relationship. As discussed in this book, there would be key signs to look for if it is a twin flame. One of them is there would more than likely be an age difference of about ten years or more. The love intensity between the both of them continues on until the end of time. They have relatively similar natures and personality styles that are complimentary for the most part. They have the same values give or take. Of course there will be slight differences in all of these aspects, but when it comes to love relationships, they want the same thing. They both admit they're comfortable being around the other. It is rare to witness couples both desiring the exact same thing, so when you have it, then be sure to never take it for granted! The ego enjoys taking everything for granted especially in love relationships.

The soul mate or twin flame connection that is long distance ultimately brings both people to live in the same city. At least one of the partners makes it happen without hesitation by moving to the same city area as their soul mate or twin flame. This process happens naturally and without force. For example, one of the partners suddenly chimes up to say they're moving to the other one's city in three months.

There are exceptions where a long distance relationship soul mate connection works. To understand if you fall into this exception rule is that you would know without a doubt this person is your lifelong mate. You both know it and stop at nothing to make it happen. This would be where one or the both of you move to the same city after getting to know one another. You develop a healthy long distance friendship before it moves into love relationship territory. You're both smart about the way you're coming together, because there is a natural ease between you. This friendship could endure for a prolonged period of time at first before you become a love item.

A healthy long term long distance connection is one where there is no consistent drama, arguing, and issues throughout it. That would be a Karmic relationship, which would need to be dissolved as the lessons have been learned. The soul mate or twin flame partner who lives in another area is a blissful contact between you both where little to no trust issues arises. This would be rather difficult considering that trust is needed for a long distance connection. Most long distance relationships do not work unless both partners set up a system where they alternate visiting one another regularly. This can be at least once a month. Over time this puts strain on less stable connections with one or both of the partners. The trust factor in a long distance connection needs to be there naturally between the partners. Ultimately both parties in the duo have plans to live with one another or live in the same town fairly soon after connecting. Nothing stops them from making that happen. The pull between the two soul mates or twin flames is incredibly strong that it's near impossible for them to not make that happen. There is no second guessing when it comes to uniting in the same city for good. These are some of the signs on how to recognize what kind of connection one might have in a long distance relationship set up.

IS THIS PERSON MY SOUL MATE?

A common question asked is, "How do I know if the person I'm with is my soul mate?"

The instant answer is that if you have to ask, then it is probably not your soul mate. It may be one of your soul mates which sift in and out of your life, but not the lifelong love soul mate. You would not need to ask this question if it is.

The longer answer is that you will need patience to see how your connection with them plays out if you're questioning if they're the big soul mate. If the person you believe to be your soul mate has chosen to break away from your connection by ending it, then you're moving into iffy territory. The way your real life long soul mate connection will work is that nothing can stop you both from making a beeline to one another. The soul connection draw is too strong and magnetic to break. Even if there is a temporary break, it does not last long because the soul connection is too strong where both mates know without a doubt that this is it for them. It's not a one-sided unrequited love. A case by case examination would need to be made as to why both partners are no longer together and yet they both hold deep attracting feelings for one another.

ATTRACTING IN THE SAME TYPES OF MATES

The soul mate connections you make throughout the course of your life are vibrational matches to you. If you attracted in someone you are constantly unhappy with for a soul mate, then come to the realization that you attracted that person and their energy to you.

I often hear others protest, "Why do I keep on attracting the same type of lover to me!?"

In order to break from that cycle, you would need to take action steps in raising your vibration in order to attract in someone of a higher caliber.

You can do this by shifting your perception and interests in life to something more positive. This takes work since human souls are innate and their basic nature stays relatively the same. The way an individual behaves is taught and learned through their upbringing and the society they live in.

Many find they go through several short term soul mate love connections that rarely have much lift off. This is to teach you important tools that prepare you for the right one. This also raises your vibration to the right ones vibration. If you do not learn from those short lived soul mate connections, then you will continue to attract in the same type of short lived soul mates to you. They are the class that preps you for the right one.

BEING TOO RIGID IN YOUR SOUL MATE SEARCH

Someone is single and looking to date, but they have the unbending list of what they're looking for in a partner. Many of the qualities on that list are of the superficial variety, such as what this potential soul mate should look like and how tall they should be, etc. This is someone allowing their ego to paint an unrealistic picture of a potential soul mate that has been airbrushed in a magazine. Falling for someone easy on the eyes does not mean it will be a lasting long term relationship. It takes more than good looks to be a stable, loving partner. You will be on the hunt for a mate indefinitely until you release this inflexibility.

This is not the only way those who fall into this category see things with such severity. Most of their choices in life are learned. It's all they know because it was all they allowed themselves to know. Anything beyond their backyard is unseen. While all human souls have certain values of what they'd like in a mate such as the person be spiritually based or not be a cigarette smoker. Rigid egotistical qualities would be that this mate must look like an Adonis model or kiss the ground you walk on daily.

While having a physical attraction to a potential partner is helpful, it will not be what keeps that person around you indefinitely. Many are guilty of it to an extent as it's what the media has shoved into the minds of human souls during the developmental stage. If the person is not tall with a tight body and six pack abs, then you will not give that person a second look. You're searching for the image of a mate who has been airbrushed and photo shopped up in a magazine. You're looking for someone who resembles the Prince or Princess that exists in popular animated fable love stories. No one stays looking that way forever no matter how well you take care of yourself. The fit people in the world eventually witness a decline in muscle and body mass as they age. Bodies are not designed to last, even though it is vital you take care of your body, mind and soul in all ways possible while you inhabit it. The truth is many human souls fall in love and end up in long term relationships with those they normally might've considered to not be their "type". They end up falling in love with that person and vice versa regardless. This is a true genuine soul attraction. It is the souls being drawn in and attracted to one another regardless that they're not what the media considers to be exceptionally perfect.

WILL A ROMANTIC FLING DELAY THE CONNECTION WITH MY LIFELONG SOUL MATE?

A brief romantic fling cannot create a hindrance in preventing your lifelong soul mate from entering the picture. Nothing can permanently stop the life partner that is intended to connect with you from doing so. If you're with someone in a mini-relationship or a fling, and then the one that you were intended to be with crosses paths with you, there is no way either of you will not notice. The pull between one another will be too strong.

Some have left marriages when they discovered they have met their one true soul mate. This is the case where they've left these relationship commitment connections for someone who ends up being their partner until they exit this lifetime. This is not the case where someone leaves their partner 'thinking' this new person is the one they're meant to be with and yet that falls apart too.

WHERE IS MY SOUL MATE? I'VE BEEN WAITING FOREVER!

When you're content with you, your life, and where you're at, then the right love partner enters the picture. If you do not love yourself, how do you expect someone else to? I've witnessed others cry out in frustration that it's been years and no love relationship. It's the frustration energy that pushes the right person away. The right person isn't going to go after someone who has frustrated energy around them. This will turn off and repel the right one. Love yourself and be comfortable with being alone, while being open and receptive to what and who may come.

HAVING ENDLESS ISSUES AND DRAMA IN YOUR CURRENT RELATIONSHIP

When you are in a healthy relationship, it will not feel like you're pushing against resistance. If you feel that you run into a roadblock with your current partner at every turn, then accept that this is how it is right now with your current partner, or choose to distance yourself from this connection. Being conflicted will not help in strengthening a love connection. In order for a relationship to thrive, you must let it go. You cannot wait for someone to come around because the odds of that happening are slim. This is not said to let you down, but the angels will not give someone false hope either. They are all about two souls working it out together. If both souls do not put in an effort to make healthy changes within the relationship, then it is likely to stay as it is.

Chapter Twelve

Friendships Change As You Evolve

When you walk down a higher spiritual path, your Guides and Angels will repel those you need to stay away from. In the process, you will attract in new people who aim for spiritual growth or who are already living in the light. Changes in your friendships are a normal process for those who frequently evolve. You find that you no longer have the same interests as those you had considered once close. When my vibration had risen to an astronomical degree from my previous way of life, I discovered that those I had once connected with were headed down a path I had no interest in. They were content to stay exactly where they are with no need for improvement. The interests they had were based purely on a superficial level. Many of them were prone to spending their days drinking, experimenting with drugs, or being a regular fixture in a bar. This used to be who I was in my twenties, but I evolved so rapidly I could no longer fake my interest in those activities. I'm not talking about the occasional get together with a buddy and a beer. This is about those who live a toxic life on a daily basis. There is no judgment of course if you revel in those activities, but when you are doing your best to live as healthy as you can while pursuing your love of spiritual or religious interests, you want to surround yourself with like minded souls as friends. I'm by no means perfect and I make mistakes just as much as anyone else. We're all works in progress.

How can you tell if your friends are true friends of integrity? When you're hanging out with your friends, are you always having an alcoholic drink or drug? If most of the time you are with them you have an alcoholic drink, then these are not real friends, but enablers. Do they prompt you to make poor life choices? They do not have to coerce you into making an unsound choice. If while in their presence you find that your negative addictions are fed, or you make repeated toxic choices, then you can be sure you're not surrounded by friends of integrity. True friends have your higher self's best interests at heart. This is not about the occasional drink you have with your friends, but rather the kinds of friends where you take on toxic vices every time you are with them, or the majority of the time you are with them. You feel temporarily fulfilled. Someone who is intoxicated pats you on your back in support when you're making an unsound choice, but their judgment is not clear. They are patting everybody on the back no matter what they're doing. This is not real love. You feed off each other's addictions and thus form a co-dependent connection. Some of this stems from fears of loneliness, a need for love, and desperation for friendships to the point where you will be friends with anybody, even if it is detrimental to your well-being. Months later, you discover that your life has been in the same place it's been in for some time. Call upon Archangel Raphael to remove any toxic addictions from your life and to help you get clear minded. Call upon Archangel Chamuel to assist you in finding friends of integrity and who are aligned with your higher self and greater good.

There was a point in my mid to late thirties where I chose to create a relationship with God and my Spirit team daily. This included working and communicating with them on a regular basis. I had finally come to the profound realization that my life before that was not as joyful as I believed it to be. I was unfulfilled by the mundane superficiality that so many were perpetuating around me. I needed more! When I invited Heaven permanently into my life and let them know we were going to develop a serious relationship, only then did I notice the positive changes in my life take place. This enabled me to not only improve my life, but help others as well. Having an understanding of where we came from has assisted me in navigating through the often challenging roads were often faced with as human souls. I chose to be mindful and cautious of who I allowed around me. I was also careful about what I was ingesting into my body including foods, alcohol, and other addictions. My mantra became either keep it in moderation or dissolve it completely. My interest in it was dropping as I moved into that space naturally. Having those around you who operate solely on a lower vibration will contaminate your aura and own positive energy. This is a perfect example of why psychic readers or anyone who works with the general public should practice shielding themselves. This is by visualizing Archangel Michael surrounding you with white light.

I was hesitant to discussing my rising spiritual interests or in opening up about how I psychically knew certain things about someone for fear of ridicule with just anyone. I did not want to announce or say the words of where I was getting my accurate information about them from. I assumed that the majority of people around me were mostly atheists or who had no belief in God, a higher power, the light or whatever one associates God to be. The main reason I assumed this was they preferred living a toxic path. They had never uttered a spiritual word as long as I had known them. This does not bother me of course, because I do not discredit good friendships simply because of a different belief system. As long as both parties are open and accepting of the other person's way of life, then there is no reason to not be friends. You need a high level of maturity to be friends with those who have differing opinions and beliefs. You would limit, avoid or keep your philosophical discussions to a minimum. However, there is a difference if they are partaking in certain deadly vices that are no longer conducive to your overall well-being. It should be common etiquette knowledge to never discuss religion or politics at a get together anyway, unless you know for sure they share your beliefs. Human souls can rarely be swayed to your belief system after one conversation. This is a personal choice they develop on their own.

For others around me I noticed that if it was not about sex or something superficial, then they could not be more bored or uninterested. This started to limit my friendships as we live in a world that is hyper-media focused. They may not be all that interested in anything beyond superficiality. This is what they have allowed their communities and peers to raise them on. It keeps them distracted and disconnected from knowing who they are and why they are here to begin with. When there is no room for anything else, then as a spiritual person you lose interest.

If I posted something on my social networking page in the realms of spirituality, then there would be one or two bad apples that would comment something patronizing about it or make a joke. I was around those that were either spiritually open or sexually open. Since I fall into both sides, if I posted something in either category I feared mockery from one or the other. I felt that I could not truly be myself and there appeared to be no room for any of it. I moved into a place of wanting to remove all traces of me on social networking sites, but then my higher self grabbed hold of the reigns. *'Wait a minute. This is my life and I'll post what I want. If you don't like it then remove yourself or I'll remove you.'*

I had to put my foot down and remove hundreds of people that I knew were going to have judgment towards the spiritual stuff or the sex stuff. These same people were around when I used to be slightly superficial myself. Although I had some measure of superficiality, the spiritual nature of who I was in truth, was present in there as well. When I shifted, I never reverted back. In fact, once the spiritual teachings blew up as part of my purpose, those friends who have been around me for years would comment that they were not surprised. They would say things like, "You always had your foot in Heaven's door for as long as I've known you. It was only a matter of time before it would blow up into this awesomeness that exists with you now." We are all unique individuals with varying concepts to share or teach. My Spirit team let me know that the right people who are more aligned with my new beliefs, and/or who are open and accepting to all of it would be attracted to me.

LONELINESS

Loneliness is a frequent protest among many human souls. They express feelings of loneliness and a lack of having any solid friendships or love relationships. This is due to a combination of several factors. The current way of life perpetuated by the media is one aspect. The rise in technology and the Internet has predominantly promoted superficiality and a lack of genuine relationship connections among humanity as a whole. It has created a larger gap and disconnect between the human soul and God. This gap has left the human soul feeling perpetually empty while craving anything that will fill the emptiness up. The soul will flip flop all over the place making poor judgment choices, such as getting involved with the wrong people to feeding their soul a toxic addiction in order to feel whole. None of this works as some have likely witnessed. The loneliness continues to be a common complaint from that soul over the years.

Loneliness is especially the case if you are going through a spiritual or major transition of some kind. The spiritual community is an open, accepting and loving group of bright souls. It is still not easy for one to form friendships whenever there is any kind of transition in your life to begin with. If you are frequently evolving then you are going through many shifts and transitions in your life. This process weeds out many of your current friendships. You must be comfortable being alone and with yourself before you can attract in new friendships. This is the same concept as searching for a soul mate. You cannot diligently search for soul mates and friendships. All REAL relationships and connections happen when you are not looking for it. They come to you naturally and effortlessly at the right time.

Loneliness is the human condition. You came into this world alone and you will leave this world alone. When you were born you were a perfect well rounded human soul experiencing joy, peace, love, in tune psychic abilities and contentment. It was society and those that raised you that inflicted all sorts of nonsense onto your soul causing you to experience negative feelings such as loneliness. Loneliness is an emptiness that cannot be cured or filled up by another human soul or filled up with addictions. The emptiness is so vast it would be outlandish to place that responsibility on another person to fill. What you are craving is God's love. It is natural for a soul to attract in a healthy companion or other half while on their journey, regardless of the gender of that soul. Yet, the attraction of that companion should not be out of filling an inner void, because this taints the union causing it to be a false connection that will end. You're basically using the other person, not because you truly love and adore them, but because you have a lacking void within you that needs to be filled. When you gain solid relationship tools and knowledge in order to function in a healthy connection whether it's a friendship or love connection, only then will you be facing in the direction of happiness.

You will also not attract in the right kind of friendships in a state of loneliness or boredom. You will attract those that are similar or worse off than you. This will leave you to fall into a deeper despair. Get happy and productive first while allowing the right friendships to come in on their own time. You will be content with this new you that you will not have the time to notice when or if the right friendships have shown up yet. Find hobbies and interests to occupy your time off so that you are not sitting on the couch all day with a beer feeling deep loneliness. Ask your Guides and Angels to work with you on removing those feelings of loneliness and to help you experience profound inner joy.

You will need to look at where you are hoping to find new friendships. Are you going to the bars to find these new friendships? Many try this avenue and end up disappointed feeling more alone. When you meet someone at a bar, the friendships are typically short lived. You are meeting those that likely partake in the same escapism as you do. This is a broad generalization, but we're not speaking in specifics. What happens when you are friends with someone who is more or less a barfly? You fall into the bell jar together delaying yourself from achieving the life you dreamed of.

Bars are a place where many dark entities lurk. These are spirits that avoided the light when they passed away. They attach themselves to the drinking patrons permanently or for a prolonged period of time. They prompt the human soul to continuously drink or do hard drugs indefinitely. They prod them to make poor life choices. This is not in judgment as I will be the first to raise my hand to say that I used to love hanging in bars in my early twenties. It was where the drinks were! There is a difference between going to a bar with a friend once in a blue moon for a drink versus going to a bar weekly or even daily. Many of the friendships you make if any are with those who love you in the moment of high intoxication, but their feelings shift when they wake up the next morning feeling gross, moody, lethargic and unfit. The only way to get rid of the feeling is to continue drinking. It's a cycle until you put your foot down that you need to keep it in moderation or give it up completely. It is no surprise that many who fit this description are starving for real friendships. You cannot attract quality friendships while in a state of addictions. You will bring in those like you, who are not the stable long term friendships you desire.

My friend's warn others not to use the word bored around me. This is because there is always something to do! To begin curbing your feelings of loneliness and boredom, discover what your true hobbies and interests are that bring you joy. Do you enjoy regular walks on the beach, certain sports, road trips or creative pursuits? The key is to choose an activity that is not negative or toxic, but rather productive and uplifting. This is where you are likely to find quality friendships. If you love painting in your spare time, then consider taking a course on painting at a trade school or college. If you love being physically active, then join softball leagues or rock climbing groups, etc. It does not matter if you already know how to do these activities, because it will get your energy out there in the right places. You will be spending several months or many weeks with the same people who have a like minded interest. They are more apt to be quality people who are productive in their lives as well. You are spending your free time wisely by engaging in something you love doing. This raises your vibration to a more joyful level, which attracts more good things into your life including great friendships!

WE ARE ALL TEACHERS

When you shift into a more spiritually minded soul, then you appreciate the connections you make with those around you. You do not take them for granted. This can be a friendship, relationship or an acquaintance. You learn something from someone that crosses paths with you because everyone is a teacher. This can be someone you met for as little as a minute. Take a look at the various people you have crossed paths with in the past. It can even be someone that cuts you off in traffic. What could that person possibly have had to teach you, you might ask. How about patience? Perhaps you are being taught to not allow the little things to affect you by remaining detached from any kind of traumatic crisis.

Examine the close relationships you formed which are long passed. It is easy to have disdain towards certain past relationships where one might have been hurt, but I don't regret any of my relationships, even the bad ones. There was knowledge I had to gain while in them as you are meant to pick up something of substance in relation to your growth. You attracted in that person at that particular time. It was designed with the goal to be of benefit for the both of you. There comes a time while in a friendship or love relationship with someone where one or both of you have served your purpose and the point becomes moot. This is when you know it is time to move on. With certain relationships, such as romantic, there can be two people who spend this entire lifetime together and act as partners in crime. They are evolving together and facing in the same direction. They gain knowledge while together as well as with those they come into contact with outside of the relationship.

DISSOLVING FRIENDSHIPS

Your true friends never ridicule or make fun of you, but instead support you. They do not place unnecessary demands on you or your time. They are flexible and know how you operate and accept this. If you have a friend that has been consistently upset over something you do or don't do, then this is a clue that it is time to consider distancing yourself from them temporarily. You may choose to dissolve the union altogether if it continues. You have different values and what you expect from the other. If you were once seeing eye-to-eye and facing the same direction, you have now hit a fork in the road embarking on separate paths with different views and interests. The purpose of your friendship has been fulfilled.

If you are negative and a gossip, then you will attract that same type of person to you. When you grow and walk a larger path, you will find that you can no longer relate to those people you initially attracted in. In fact, you find them to be energy zappers where you are drained after having a phone conversation with them. You become fully aware of your surroundings and how they have contributed to your negative state. You realize how miserable you are with them only to discover that you played a part in it too.

The only way to start attracting friendships with greater people is to begin the process of improving yourself first. There will be a transition period that could last anywhere from one to three years as you work on yourself in a big way. During this transition, some of your previous friendships will begin fading and newer improved friendships will gradually enter your life. There will be some friendships that might be difficult to dissolve. These friends may be the biggest energy zappers of them all. They feed on you like a vampire. They have their clutches in you and have no desire to let go. Pay no mind or attention to this. It's not your responsibility to be the source of happiness for someone else. Ask Archangel Raguel to assist you in peacefully dissolving the friendships and relationships that consistently cause you grief.

There were friendships I had in the past where I was not comfortable with in discussing my spiritual pursuits and the profound changes that were happening within me. You never share your dreams with those you have to convince. If people are critical, then it will shut down your Heavenly connections and block your communication with God. Their ridicule will affect your self-esteem and lower your vibration. I had friends who might not understand my spiritual beliefs, but were delighted to hear about it. Most people find that they are curious or fascinated by it because there is something about it that reminds them of who they once were in the Spirit world. It triggers a past life or spirit world memory and offers them comfort. They could be at a point in their life where nothing around them matters anymore. They feel trapped in their body unable to connect to anything. There were others who never uttered a word of spirituality, but grew to be interested in that realm after hearing my teachings. They miraculously expanded into that world in an even bigger way.

My interests in certain friendships and people were changing as I walked down this higher path. Doors were opening and relationships were shifting by ending or improving. It was a period of adjustment and I would have previously approached that kicking and screaming, but instead it was a peaceful transition. I found those that were part of religious institutions had taken more of a liking towards me than atheists did. I was initially surprised by this, since I was formerly under the assumption or façade that those who had no spiritual belief system were more open minded than those who were religious. Even though religious and spiritual beliefs vary in certain areas, we found some common denominators when it came to circumstances like an afterlife, God, Heaven and angels. I sat with a religious couple over a dinner. They later commented to someone we mutually knew at how awestruck they were with me. They were blown away and moved by what I spoke about. There is familiar ground in varying spiritual belief systems if people remain open.

I've made enemies for being open about my beliefs. I've had people who volunteered to write me out of the blue through a social networking page and say, "Wow, I realize that I don't like you at all." They would then delete and block me. They were surprisingly atheists, who as stated, I thought would be more open than someone who was religious. I found the opposite to be the case in my personal experience. You ignore it and forge on with your purpose in merging with the Light. The Light will ensure all of your needs are met. It will ensure you are around good-hearted, compassionate and understanding people who you feel comfortable around. The angels will deter those who are a danger for you to be around and extricate them out of your vicinity. A person such as this is consumed by toxic energy and rules their life predominately through their ego. You being a sensitive and in tune to your surroundings will soak that up like a dirty dish rag. Meanwhile, in the works are greater more important human souls operating from a higher place entering your vicinity. They are drawn to you as you make the shift onto a higher level of consciousness. This process takes quite a bit of time because you're growing and evolving at a rapid pace. There are people exiting your life much more slowly.

You will be hesitant to dissolving certain friendships because you do care about them and the good times you had, but at the same time they are not welcoming or responsive towards your new beliefs. They are living unhealthy lives that no longer jive with who you are becoming. You may choose to make yourself less available to them until they have moved into your acquaintance box. Before you know it, you will be communicating less and less. Some of these friendships and relationships might be with people who are heavily into negative substances and addictions. Long before you've made that spiritual shift, you were likely working on lifestyle changes gradually. This includes what you consume and shove into your body. You find the new friendships you make are with those open to what you believe in, even if they do not partake in it or fully understand it. Those unions are more beautiful, loving, and improved than you could have imagined with anybody else. They are pure and full of light. An uplifting energy is created when both of your soul lights are together. You surpassed a superficial mundane existence and expanded your consciousness.

My friendships changed to a great degree as my newfound interests moved onto a whole new level. Some shifted comfortably with my heightened interest. They effortlessly accepted this is the new me and not some whimsical fly by hobby. I have eternally changed and continue to do so. This is the same concept as those who claim to be born again Christians. They might have run into friendships that no longer shared their beliefs or talked it down. One of the differences may be is that my reason for letting people go is because they were not serving my higher purpose. They were not supportive or they ridiculed my rising interests of a healthier variety. Archangel Michael is by my side on a daily basis and he extracts those from my vicinity, often before I'm aware that they are close.

The spiritual transition I made in the past was empowering, but there was an immense amount of alone time because I was no longer interested in those I was previously connecting with. I was in an area where there were certain types of people I would experience a connection with. If I felt isolated before, then I felt inaccessible and disconnected from everyone during the transition. This is a normal and typical part of the process where your personal life might seem unfulfilling. You are removing your previous old way of life in order to bring in new people on your level.

I would continue to be approached and many would express great interest towards me, but I felt emptiness with them. I would wonder how long in before it was time for me to mention my spiritual interests, and then how quickly the judgment or skepticism would fall over their face. I knew that I would have to remain in the spiritual closet until it was safe to open up about it with the right people. It was generally not that long before I'd know whether or not someone would be in a place to hear it and understand. I had discussed it with certain friends who I assumed were spiritually inclined, but found that it would go through one ear and out the other. This would be the case whenever I would share the profound changes that were happening with me. It was as if they did not buy it or believe it, so they opted to ignore that it was said. I could tell by meeting someone who would be open to it after a few sentences spoken from their mouth.

I knew love and romance was going to be more of a challenge, as this person would have to completely understand. They would not have to partake in it or do the things I do, but that person would have to be open minded, supportive and loving about it. What I do and what I experience with this is not up for a debate. I knew there would be no way I could be involved with a non-believer because this is something I do every day now. I would need to communicate openly with the one I'm with. How could I do that if it would be subjected to ridicule? If you find yourself in that predicament, then ask your Guides and Angels to send you someone who is open and receptive to what you do without judgment. This is someone who is walking a spiritual path. I would first ask that they open up the mind of the person I'm with before making any sudden movements. This was not the only reason I chose to be alone. The portal was open into this new way of life and I was fascinated and immersed in study and research as I perfected the gifts I already had.

Never divulge your dreams or deepest interests to anyone you suspect to be untrustworthy or a negative naysayer. Guard your dreams and aspirations with delicacy. Don't blurt out your closest secrets to an unreliable soul. You can tell by the response you get from someone whether or not they support you, or if they are operating purely from ego. One who supports and coaxes you on with your dream is the real deal. Someone who always belittles you, or responds negatively to your dreams, should be dissolved out of your life. With all of the wonderful people in the world it's important not to waste one minute with someone who has issues about you, or who is jealous of you and the attention you receive.

I am impossible to control, which is another sign of spiritual progress. I act and function in complete independence. I do not follow the crowd and always had separate views that were not on par with the majority. No attention on my part is paid to how others feel about it. I've had friends in the past that were uncomfortable that I own my life. They would find some way to undercut something about me. They would say it as a backhanded compliment as if I wouldn't notice. Today, I no longer become friends with unsupportive people. Being in tune, you're able to asses that energy in the beginning rather than knee deep into the connection. I'm not this way with others because I live in a higher frequency than they do. Those types of personalities were disbanded out of my life. My detector is incredibly tuned in where I sense this energy immediately. There were those unaware of their lack of tact. I would continue to keep them around, but not hesitate to correct them on their naivety. Only allow those with the highest of integrity near you.

Friendships have to be earned and should

never be immediate. This applies to romantic relationships as well. You attract friendships to you the way you attract anything, through the laws of attraction. If you are at a certain level of growth you will only attract those that mirror your intent. If you're consuming negative substances such as drugs and alcohol, what types of people do you think you're going to attract in? You're not going to attract in someone walking in the light. If you find that you have on that rare occasion, then there is a reason for it. The reason is that person who is a spiritual being was guided to you by Heaven. They see you are ready to grow out of your current phase. The wonderful spiritual being is your teacher and will not be around you forever if you abuse it. When they leave you prematurely, then you may continue down your path of self-sabotage and destruction. You are given an Earth Angel to cross your path to help you, and wake up and progress your soul. There are many out there threading through the world to get you to wake up and walk the path of love, joy and peace. It is important to recognize who they are.

Archangel Chamuel and Archangel Raguel

Archangel Chamuel is referred to as, *'the finding angel'*. He can help you find anything from the right career, love partner, home or even your keys! Chamuel works with the Romance Angels when someone longs for or wishes for a loving, soul mate relationship or new friendships that are more aligned with your higher values and beliefs. He will only bring you those that are positively beneficial to you. If your twin flame is living in this lifetime with you, he can assist you both in uniting while having the courage to speak to one another. Chamuel sparks new passion and interest into current relationships. This also applies to married/committed couples who are having issues. Before you can attract in a new career or partnership, it is first important to love and believe in yourself. Archangel Chamuel is all about the love and can infuse God's love into a cold heart. He will awaken your heart chakra if it is blocked and help you to attract in love. Call upon

Archangel Chamuel if you need help finding the right love partner and friendships.

Archangel Raguel is instrumental in harmonizing relationships of all types, whether it is friendships, love or business connections. If any discord arises with your relationships with others, ask him to help you balance, elevate, smooth and mend the connection. Fighting injustice, wanting harmony and a fair resolution are other areas in which Archangel Raguel can assist you. You cannot get away with treating others badly as Archangel Raguel will come in and correct your behavior.

One thing to note is that Archangel Raguel will not get rid of a love interest you are having trouble with, but rather will enter the situation to help you see it in a new light that benefits everyone involved. This is not the case if your significant other is abusive, but rather when misunderstandings arise with no hope for solution. He rushes in to infuse his light in the situation by merging both of your souls to a place of understanding and love.

Spirit Guides and Angels

How often do you find yourself thinking about nothing in particular when suddenly a jolt of clear-cut information flies through your mind? What you receive is so commanding you experience a surge of uplifting joy coursing through all of the cells in your body. The idea, key or answer you gained was the missing piece of the puzzle to something you needed to know at that particular time. How many times have you received a nudge to do something that would positively change your life? Instead of taking action on it, you deny it chalking it off to wishful thinking. You later discover that it was indeed an answered prayer, if only you had taken notice and followed the guidance. These are some examples of how you can tell when it is your Spirit Guide or Guardian Angel communicating with you. When you get your lower self and ego out of the way, then that is when the profound answer you had been hoping for is revealed to you. The impression you acquire is so powerful that it pulls you out of the darkness you were previously stuck in. It is a bright light shining its focus directly onto the message in unadorned view. It is crystal clear as if it had been there all along and you wonder why you had not noticed it before.

There are so many joyless faces out there waiting, complaining or praying for a miracle. Instead you choose to fill your days up partaking in activities that only erode your self-esteem and overall well-being. These activities can be something you are not aware of such as sitting in traffic completely tense. You experience another mundane routine day screaming for an escape from this prison of a life you have created. You stay unhappy in your jobs, the places you live in and with certain friendships or relationships. You ponder over not having that home of your dreams or sharing your life with someone in a loving relationship. The days having this dull mindset turn into months and years with no miracle in sight. This disappointment grows like mold causing you to appear and feel eternally glum, negative and bitter. The emotional traits mask your dissatisfaction and heartbreak attracting more of that stuff to you. To cope you drown those nasty emotions with addictions from drinking heavily, ingesting chemicals, doing drugs or by partaking in time wasting activities such as gossip and Internet surfing.

You choose to be disconnected living behind a wall built of your own attitude and yet it is in your basic human nature to want to connect to other human souls, to someone, or something. You want to be happy, but that state can feel so out of reach and unobtainable you drown in its thoughts. Our way of communicating today is primarily through phone, texting, email and social networking. Even if you truly wanted to sit face-to-face you are too busy or worn out to bother. You were not intended to live your life in misery and unhappiness. For some reason, you choose to fall into a pattern of suffering. Human souls as a whole are to blame for this design.

It is never too late to improve your life. What you are looking for is right in front of you and closer than you think. Strengthen your faith and believe in the power of what exists outside of your human body. This will bring you closer to the happiness that resides within. God, your angels, spirit guides and all in Heaven can and want to assist you out of this hopelessness. They are always present around you. They want to lift you out of your life of desolation. It is irrelevant what your beliefs are and whether you are religious or an atheist. It does not matter what race you were born into in this lifetime. Nor does it matter if you are rich or poor, gay or straight, liberal or conservative. Whatever you agreed to come into this lifetime as, you are loved equally. No one is more special than anyone else. God and the angels see each of your inner lights, your innocence and your true purpose for being here. If you have veered long off course, they can help you get back to where you need to be. Who you are is a perfect child of God and love no matter where you are from or who you are.

Love Related Books by Kevin Hunter

Soul Mates and Twin Flames, Twin Flame Soul Connections, Love Party of One, Jagger's Revolution

ALSO BY KEVIN HUNTER

Warrior of Light
Empowering Spirit Wisdom
Darkness of Ego
Realm of the Wise One
Transcending Utopia
Reaching for the Warrior Within
Spirit Guides and Angels
Soul Mates and Twin Flames
Raising Your Vibration
Divine Messages for Humanity
Connecting with the Archangels
Monsters and Angels
The Seven Deadly Sins
Love Party of One
Twin Flame Soul Connections
A Beginner's Guide to the Four Psychic Clair Senses
Attracting in Abundance
Tarot Card Meanings
Abundance Enlightenment
Living for the Weekend
Ignite Your Inner Life Force
Awaken Your Creative Spirit
The Essential Kevin Hunter Collection

The Essential Kevin Hunter Collection
Available in Paperback and E-book

THE ESSENTIAL
KEVIN HUNTER
COLLECTION

Featuring the following books:
Warrior of Light, Empowering Spirit Wisdom, Darkness of Ego, Spirit Guides and Angels, Soul Mates and Twin Flames, Raising Your Vibration, Divine Messages for Humanity, and Connecting with the Archangels.

Attracting in Abundance

Opening the Divine Gates to Inviting in Blessings and Prosperity Through Body, Mind, and Soul Spirit

When you hear the word abundance, you may equate it to being blessed with a plentiful overflowing amount of money that equates to a big lottery win. Having enough money to survive comfortably enough on this physical plane is part of obtaining abundance, but it's not the destination and purpose to thrive for. You could work hard to make enough money to the point you are set for life, but that won't necessarily equate to happiness. Achieving a content satisfied state of joy and serenity starts with examining your soul's state and overall well-being. When that's in place, then the rest will follow.

Attracting in Abundance combines practical and spirit wisdom surrounding the nature of abundance. This is something that most everyone can get on board with because all human beings desire physical comforts, blessings, and prosperity, regardless of their personal values and belief systems. *Attracting in Abundance* is broken up into three parts to help move you towards inviting abundance into your life on all levels. "Part One" contains some no-nonsense lectures surrounding the philosophies, concepts, and debates on the laws of attracting in abundance. "Part Two" is the largest of the sections geared towards fine tuning the soul into preparing for abundance. "Part Three" is the final lesson plan to help crack open the gates of abundance with various helpful tidbits, guidance, and messages as well as the blocks that can prevent abundance from coming in.

WARRIOR OF LIGHT

Messages from my Guides and Angels

There are legions of angels, spirit guides, and departed loved ones in heaven that watch and guide you on your journey here on Earth. They are around to make your life easier and less stressful. Learn how you can recognize the guidance of your own Spirit team of guides and angels around you. Author, Kevin Hunter, relays heavenly guided messages about getting humanity, the world, and yourself into shape. He delivers the guidance passed onto him by his own Spirit team on how to fine tune your body, soul and raise your vibration. Doing this can help you gain hope and faith in your own life in order to start attracting in more abundance.

EMPOWERING SPIRIT WISDOM

A Warrior of Light's Guide on Love, Career and the Spirit World

Kevin Hunter relays heavenly, guided messages for everyday life concerns with his book, *Empowering Spirit Wisdom*. Some of the topics covered are your soul, spirit and the power of the light, laws of attraction, finding meaningful work, transforming your professional and personal life, navigating through the various stages of dating and love relationships, as well as other practical affirmations and messages from the Archangels. Kevin Hunter passes on the sensible wisdom given to him by his own Spirit team in this inspirational book.

DARKNESS OF EGO

In *Darkness of Ego*, author Kevin Hunter infuses some of the guidance, messages, and wisdom he's received from his Spirit team surrounding all things ego related. The ego is one of the most damaging culprits in human life. Therefore, it is essential to understand the nature of the beast in order to navigate gracefully out of it when it spins out of control. Some of the topics covered in *Darkness of Ego* are humanity's destruction, mass hysteria, karmic debt, and the power of the mind, heaven's gate, the ego's war on love and relationships, and much more.

REACHING FOR THE WARRIOR WITHIN

Reaching for the Warrior Within is the author's personal story recounting a volatile childhood. This led him to a path of addictions, anxiety and overindulgence in alcohol, drugs, cigarettes and destructive relationships. As a survival mechanism, he split into many different "selves". He credits turning his life around, not by therapy, but by simultaneously paying attention to the messages he has been receiving from his Spirit team in Heaven since birth.

REALM OF THE WISE ONE

In the Spirit Worlds and the dimensions that exist, reside numerous kingdoms that house a plethora of Spirits that inhabit various forms. One of these tribes is called the Wise Ones, a darker breed in the spirit realm who often chooses to incarnate into a human body one lifetime after another for important purposes.

The *Realm of the Wise One* takes you on a magical journey to the spirit world where the Wise Ones dwell. This is followed with in-depth and detailed information on how to recognize a human soul who has incarnated from the Wise One Realm. Author, Kevin Hunter, is a Wise One who uses the knowledge passed onto him by his Spirit team of Guides and Angels to relay the wisdom surrounding all things Wise One. He discusses the traits, purposes, gifts, roles, and personalities among other things that make up someone who is a Wise One. Wise Ones have come in the guises of teachers, shaman, leaders, hunters, mediums, entertainers and others. *Realm of the Wise One* is an informational guide devoted to the tribe of the Wise Ones, both in human form and on the other side.

TRANSCENDING UTOPIA

Available in Paperback and E-book

Transcending Utopia is packed with practical and spirit knowledge that focuses on enhancing your life through empowering divinely guided spiritual related teachings, inspiration, wisdom, guidance, and messages. The way to accelerate existence on Earth towards Utopia is if every person on the planet resided in their soul's true nature, which is in a state of all love, joy, and peace. The ultimate Nirvana is surpassing that perfection through methods that a limited consciousness could ever dream possible. This is the exceptional glory your soul was born into before the dense turbulence of Earthly life enveloped and suffocated you.

Transcending Utopia is to go beyond your limits and travel outside of the generic mundane materialistic achievement that human beings taught one another to thrive for. A utopian society is where everything is perfectly blissful on all levels according to the sanctified values you were born with. The sensations connected to how flawless everything feels in that moment reveals the authentic perfection you were made from. Utopia is the ideal paradise as imagined in one's dreams that seems to be inaccessible by human standards. It is a state of mind that is possible to reach by adopting broader ways of looking at circumstances while being disciplined about how you conduct your life. You search for a sign of this utopia through external means, only to be consistently left with disappointment. This is because utopia begins and ends inside the spark that burns within your spirit like a pilot light waiting to be ignited.

Living for the Weekend

The Winding Road Towards Balancing Career Work and Spiritual Life

Available in Paperback and E-book

Working hard to ensure your bills are paid can leave your soul spiritually starved for soul nourishment. When your ultimate goal is to obtain enough money to be comfortable that you become carried away in that current, then there is little to no room for Divine enrichment.

Many work to survive in jobs they hate because it's the way it is. As a result, they experience and endure all sorts of emotional pain whether it is through depression, sadness, anger, or any other kind of negative stressor. Some silently suffer through this emotional strain gradually killing off their life force. If you don't have a healthy social life and positive fun filled activities and hobbies to balance that burden outside of that, then that could add additional tension. What's it all for if you can't live the life you've always wanted to live? Instead, you spend your days growing forever miserable and broken.

Living for the Weekend examines the pitfalls, struggles, as well as the benefits available in the current modern day working world. This is followed up with spiritual and practical tips, guidance, messages, and discussions on ways to incorporate more balance and enlightenment to a cutthroat material driven world.

MONSTERS AND ANGELS

An Empath's Guide to Finding Peace in a Technologically Driven World Ripe with Toxic Monsters and Energy Draining Vampires

Every person on the planet is capable of being empathic and sensitive, to becoming an energy vampire or toxic monster. No one is exempt from displaying the darker sides of their ego. The easiest and most efficient way to spread any kind of energy is online. Every time you log onto the Internet, there is a larger chance you're going to see something related to the news, media, or gossip areas thrown in front of you, even if you attempt to avoid it as much as possible. You're absorbing everything that your consciousness faces, including the ugly and the wicked, which has its own consequences. This tempestuous energy is tossed into the Universe ultimately creating a flame-throwing battleground inside and around you.

Monsters and Angels discusses how technology, media, and social media have an immense power in distributing both positive and negative influences far and wide. This is about being mindful of what can negatively affect your state of being, and how to counter and avoid that when and wherever possible. This is why it's beneficial to govern yourself, your life, and your surroundings like a strict disciplined executive.

Twin Flame Soul Connections

Recognizing the Split Apart, the Truths and Myths of Twin Flames, Soul Love Connections, Soul Mates, and Karmic Relationships

Twin Flames have a shared ongoing sentiment and quest from the moment they're a spark shooting out of God's love that explodes into a blinding white fire that breaks apart causing one to be two, until two become one again, separate and whole, and back around again. Looking into the eyes of your Twin Flame is like looking into the eyes of God, because to know love is to know God.

When one thinks of a Soul Mate or Twin Flame, they might equate it to a passionate romantic relationship where you're making love on a white sandy palm tree lined beach in paradise for the rest of your lives. This beautiful mythological notion has caused great turmoil in others who long for this person that fits the description of a lothario character in a romance novel. It is also an unrealistic and misguided interpretation of the Soul Mate or Twin Flame dynamic.

Twin Flame Soul Connections discusses and lists some of the various myths and truths surrounding the Twin Flames, and how to identify if you've come into contact with your Twin Flame, or if you know someone who has. The ultimate goal is not to find ones Twin Flame, but to awaken ones heart to love, and to work on becoming complete and whole as an individual soul through spiritual self-mastery, life lessons, growth, and raising your consciousness. Your soul's life was born out of love and will die right back into that love.

IGNITE YOUR INNER LIFE FORCE

Ignite Your Inner Life Force is an introduction guide for teens, young adults, and anyone seeking answers, messages, and guidance and surrounding spiritual empowerment. This is from understanding what Heaven, the soul, and spiritual beings are to knowing when you are connecting with your Spirit team of Guides and Angels. Some of the topics covered are communicating with Heaven, working with your Spirit team, what your higher self is, your life purpose and soul contract, what the ego is, love and relationships, your vibration energy, shifting your consciousness and thinking for yourself even when you stand alone. This is an in-depth primer manual offering you foundation as you find a higher purpose navigating through your personal journey in today's modern day practical world.

AWAKEN YOUR CREATIVE SPIRIT

Your creative spirit is more than being artistic and getting involved in creativity pursuits, although this is a good part of it. When your creative spirit is activated by a high vibration state of being, then this is the space you create from. You can apply this to your dealings in life, your creative and artistic pursuits, and to having a greater communication line with your Spirit team on the Other Side. *Awaken Your Creative Spirit* is an overview of what it means to have access to Divine assistance and how that plays a part in arousing the muse within you in order to bring your state of mind into a happier space.

The *Warrior of Light* series of pocket books are available in paperback and E-book called, *Spirit Guides and Angels, Soul Mates and Twin Flames, Divine Messages for Humanity, Raising Your Vibration, Connecting with the Archangels*, and *The Seven Deadly Sins*

TAROT CARD MEANINGS

A Beginner's Guide to the
FOUR PSYCHIC CLAIR SENSES

Learn about the four main psychic clair senses to help you connect with Heaven, the Spirit World, and the Other Side. Take that one step further and use those senses to read the Tarot! *Tarot Card Meanings* is an encyclopedia reference guide that takes the Tarot apprentice reader through each of the 78 Tarot Cards offering the potential general meanings and interpretations that could be applied when conducting a reading, whether it be spiritual, love, general, or work related questions. This is an easy to understand manual for the Tarot novice that is having trouble interpreting cards for themselves, or a Tarot reader who loves the craft and is looking for a refresher or another point of view. The *Four Psychic Clair Senses* focuses on the main channels that Heaven and Spirit communicate with you. *Both books are available in Paperback and E-book wherever books are sold.*

Available in Paperback and E-Book
is the B-Side to the Attracting in Abundance book

ABUNDANCE ENLIGHTENMENT

An Easy Motivational Guide to
the Laws of Attracting in Abundance
and Transforming Your Soul

Ultimate authentic success surrounds your soul's growth and evolving process. It's when you realize that none of the physical ego driven desires matter in the end. You can work hard to make sure you stay afloat, you're able to pay your bills, and support yourself and family, but you're not chasing popularity for external validation. Any amount of goodness displayed from your heart is the true measure of real accomplishment.

An overflowing feeling of optimism and love coupled with faith and action is what increases the chances of attracting good things and positive experiences to you. Abundance is more than monetary and financial increase. It can also be about reaching an optimistic well-being state of joy, peace, and love. This positive emotional mindful state simultaneously attracts in blessings.

Abundance Enlightenment is the follow up book to *Attracting in Abundance*. It contains both practical guidance and spirit wisdom that can be applied to everyday life. Some of the key topics surround the laws of attraction as well as healthier money management and improving your soul to help make you a fine tuned in abundance attractor.

About Kevin Hunter

Kevin Hunter is the metaphysical spiritual author of more than two-dozen spiritually based books that tackle a variety of genres and tend to have a strong male protagonist. The messages and themes he weaves in his work surround Spirit's own communications of love and respect, which he channels and infuses into his writing work. His spiritually based empowerment books include *Warrior of Light, Empowering Spirit Wisdom, Realm of the Wise One, Reaching for the Warrior Within, Darkness of Ego, Transcending Utopia, Living for the Weekend, Ignite Your Inner Life Force, Awaken Your Creative Spirit,* and *Tarot Card Meanings.* His metaphysical pocket books series include, *Spirit Guides and Angels, Soul Mates and Twin Flames, Raising Your Vibration, Divine Messages for Humanity, Connecting with the Archangels, The Seven Deadly Sins, Four Psychic Clair Senses, Monsters and Angels, Twin Flame Soul Connections, Attracting in Abundance,* and *Abundance Enlightenment.* He is also the author of the dating singles guide *Love Party of One*, the horror/drama, *Paint the Silence*, and the modern day erotic love story, *Jagger's Revolution.*

Kevin started out in the entertainment business in 1996 as the personal development guy to one of Hollywood's most respected talent, Michelle Pfeiffer, for her boutique production company, Via Rosa Productions. She dissolved her company after several years and he made a move into coordinating film productions for the studios on such films as *One Fine Day, A Thousand Acres, The Deep End of the Ocean, Crazy in Alabama, The Perfect Storm, Original Sin, Harry Potter & the Sorcerer's Stone, Dr. Dolittle 2,* and *Carolina.* He considers himself a beach bum born and raised in Southern California. For more information: www.kevin-hunter.com